RUGBY WORLD CUP 2011

THE OFFICIAL GUIDE

First published by Carlton Books Limited 2011
Copyright © 2011 Carlton Books Limited

The words "Rugby World Cup" are protected by Trade Mark
and/or Copyright.
TM © Rugby World Cup Limited 1986–2011. All rights reserved.
RWC Font. Copyright © 2008 RWC Ltd. All rights reserved.
Unauthorised use, modification, reproduction and distribution prohibited.
TM © Rugby World Cup Limited 1986–2011. All rights reserved.

Carlton Books Limited
20 Mortimer Street
London, W1T 3JW

A CIP catalogue record for this book is available from the British Library.
10 9 8 7 6 5 4 3 2 1

ISBN: 978-1-84732-818-2

Printed in Dubai

Senior Editor: Conor Kilgallon
Project Art Editor: Luke Griffin
Designer: Sailesh Patel
Picture Research: Paul Langan
Production: Maria Petalidou

At the time of going to press, the
guide is correct for all match
venues. For any updates, please
visit www.rugbyworldcup.com

All statistics are correct at
1 February 2011.

About the Author:
Chris Hawkes grew up supporting the
English Premiership team, the Leicester
Tigers, and played rugby at junior county
level before going on to play professional
cricket for Leicestershire CCC. He was
editor of the bestselling *Cricketer's Who's
Who* annual for a number of years and has
gone on to write a number of books on
rugby, football and cricket, including the
Rugby World Cup 2007 Guide.

RUGBY WORLD CUP 2011

THE OFFICIAL GUIDE

Chris Hawkes

Foreword by
Bernard Lapasset
IRB Chairman

CARLTON

Contents

Introduction

Rugby wanted a World Cup. By the late 1980s it was no longer enough to be the winners of the then Five Nations Championship or be the dominant team in the southern hemisphere. What players and fans alike wanted was to be given the honour of being the champions of the world. And, in 1987, the game got its wish.

When talk of staging a Rugby World Cup was discussed in the early 1980s the main concern was the effect such a Tournament would have on the strict amateur principles by which the game had been run for over a century. Those in favour of a Rugby World Cup knew Rugby would not survive without it (football, after all, had been staging a World Cup since 1930); those against a Rugby World Cup knew the game would end up having to abandon its amateur status and would change forever. Both arguments turned out to be right: Rugby – the game, its players and its fans – needed the grand stage and the history-making moments such a Tournament provides and, in 1995, less than a decade after the first-ever Rugby World Cup, with its profile at an all-time high (helped by the staggering presence of New Zealand's Jonah Lomu and South Africa's heart-warming victory), the Game had turned professional. Not only that, the Tournament had evolved into one of the biggest and best-loved sporting events on the planet.

RWC 2011, the seventh staging of the event, promises to be the best yet and one packed with an array of intriguing possibilities. Can hosts New Zealand end what is fast becoming the most talked-about drought in world rugby –24 years without a title? Can South Africa become the first team in history to defend their World Championship crown? Can Australia become the first team to lift the Trophy for the third time? Can England repeat their heroics of RWC 2003 – the last time the Tournament was staged in the southern hemisphere? Or will France find the consistency that has so far eluded them and dismiss the painful memory of losing two Finals? And what of the minnows: can Namibia find a winning formula for the first time and how will Tournament-newcomers Russia fare?

Rugby World Cup 2011: The Official Guide provides insights into those questions and much more. With profiles on each of the 20 participating teams, features on a selection of the Tournament's potential stars, a review of the previous six Tournaments, a guide to how the countries qualified, a detailed look at the Tournament's venues, tips for tourists and enough statistics and facts to satisfy even the most curious of minds, it is essential reading for every Rugby fan who wants to be in the know when the Tournament kicks off.

South Africa's Bakkies Botha wins the line out in the Rugby World Cup 2007 Final against England.

Foreword

In 1987 the Game entered an exciting new world with the kick-off of the first ever Rugby World Cup in New Zealand and Australia. Little did we know that this historic Tournament would change the face of the Game forever, delivering the catalyst for incredible evolution, development and growth.

Although played on the same fields, New Zealand 2011 will be a far cry from those pioneering days and the humble beginnings of our showcase event. The values of respect, fair play and camaraderie that are central to the Game are as prominent as ever, but over the past 24 years Rugby World Cup has become an internationally renowned event that reaches out to all corners of the world through comprehensive media and broadcast coverage and a united passion for the Game.

There is little doubt that this Tournament, the seventh chapter of the remarkable Rugby World Cup story, will be an incredible success. Anticipation is at fever pitch and New Zealand is ready to roll out the welcome mat and become a nation of four million hosts for what will be the largest event ever hosted in this Rugby mad country.

What awaits for the 20 teams and over 85,000 overseas fans coming to New Zealand is a unique experience that will bring together a blend of world-class Rugby, superb venues and hospitality and a nationwide cultural festival celebrating the best that New Zealand has to offer. It is an event not to be missed.

For the International Rugby Board and the Game this showcase Tournament plays a much greater role than delivering a sporting spectacle. Rugby World Cup plays a central role in the development of world Rugby as the revenue provides the financial platform for the global growth of the Game.

Between 2009 and 2012 the IRB will have invested over £150 million (€79 million; ZAR 1.74 billion) in strategic high performance programmes, tournaments and grants to increase the competitiveness of the Game around the world. The aim is to have more teams capable of winning Rugby World Cup as the competitiveness of the international Game increases.

On behalf of the IRB I would like to wish you all a wonderful and memorable Rugby World Cup experience and thank you all for your tremendous support for Rugby all around the world.

Bernard Lapasset
Chairman, International Rugby Board

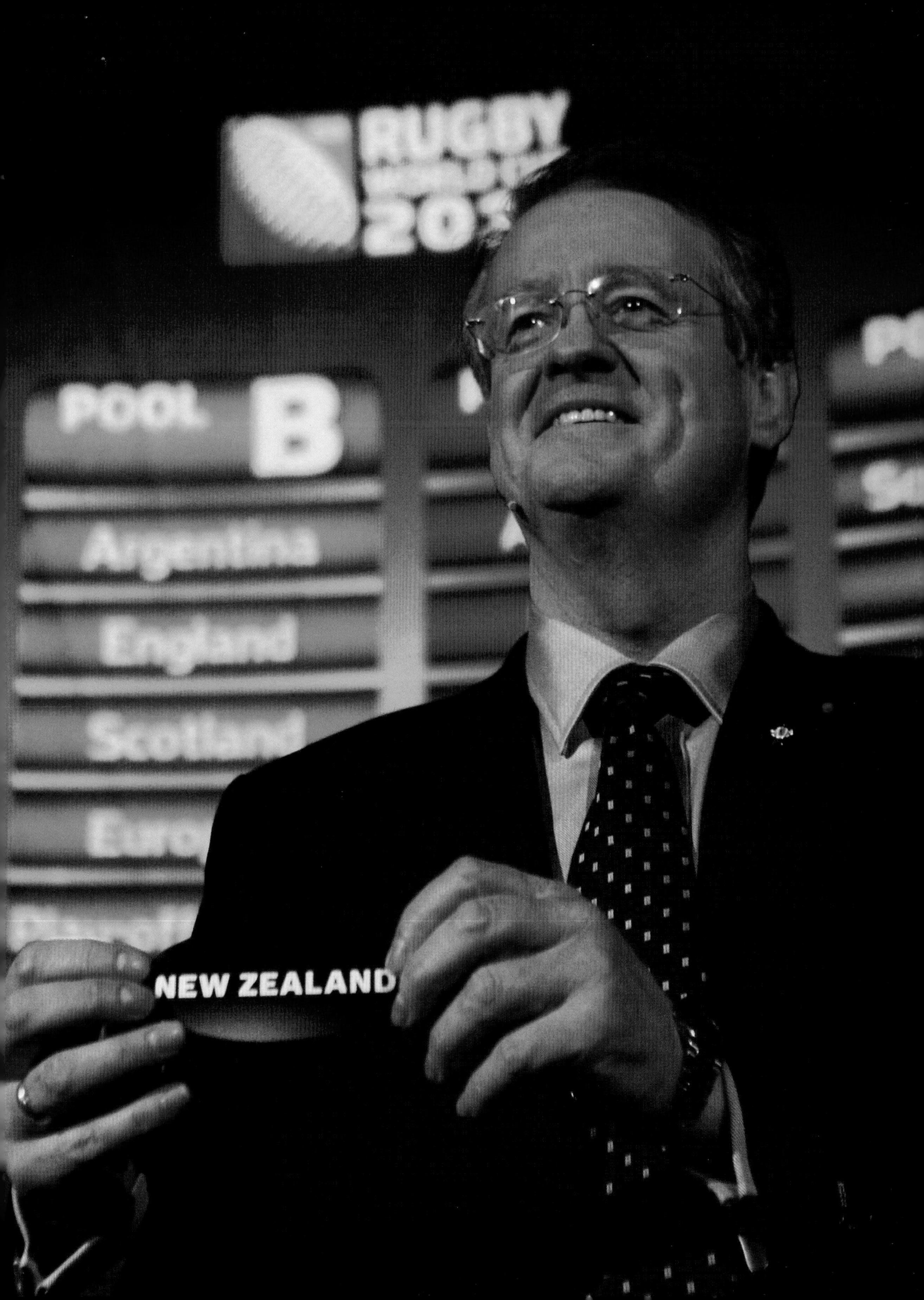
RUGBY
POOL B
Argentina
England
Scotland
NEW ZEALAND

WELCOME TO NEW ZEALAND

In 2011, for the first time since the inaugural Tournament was held in the country in 1987, Rugby World Cup will make a welcome return to New Zealand, the 'Land of the Long White Cloud', with its stunningly diverse terrain – from the subtropical golden-sand beaches of the Bay of Islands in the North Island to the windswept high-alpine peaks of the Southern Alps in the South Island – and its unbridled passion for the game of rugby. New Zealand has a rich history in the sport: the All Blacks have established a fearsome reputation over the years. The game's biggest Tournament – which will be staged in 13 venues across the country – could have found no better stage.

New Zealand is a country of vibrant cities and stunning landscapes, such as the peaks of Mount Cook in the Southern Alps.

About Rugby World Cup 2011

Looking forward to its seventh staging, Rugby World Cup has blossomed into one of the world's great sporting events, with a global television audience of four billion (RWC 2007) and 85,000 fans from more than 100 countries expected to attend one or more of the 48 matches. It is the biggest sporting event in 2011 and the largest event ever hosted in New Zealand.

The major stumbling block had been that, because a Tournament of such status would have to be run by commercial operators, it would challenge the amateur principles upon which the Game had been founded for over a century. The nay-sayers, principally those from the Home Nations (England, Ireland, Scotland and Wales), feared that a Rugby World Cup would change the Game irrevocably … and not for the better.

Not everyone agreed. Australia and New Zealand continued to push the idea and in 1983 and 1984 put forward proposals to the International Rugby Board (IRB) to host the Tournament. The

IRB instigated a feasibility study: Australia and New Zealand formed a working party and presented their findings to the IRB in Paris on 20 and 21 March 1985. The outcome of that meeting would change the Game forever.

Voting on the concept of a Rugby World Cup has become part of the Game's folklore. Australia and New Zealand had the full support of France; the Home Nations, on the other hand, remained resolutely opposed to the principle. But South Africa still had to vote. Despite (or in spite of) the fact that, as a result of their government's policy of apartheid, they faced a long period of isolation

from international sport, South Africa voted in favour of the concept. It left voting locked at 4–4 … and stalemate. The process started all over again. First England rescinded, then the Welsh delegate changed his mind and the die had been cast. The first Rugby World Cup, to be hosted jointly by Australia and New Zealand, the event's pioneers, would take place in 1987.

The first competition was a cautious, invitation-only affair, but by the last Tournament, staged in France, it had developed into a truly global phenomenon. The old-boys' mentality of the inaugural event was long gone: 91

England and France line up before the start of their semi-final showdown at Rugby World Cup 2007 at the Stade de France, Paris.

nations from all five continents attempted to qualify for the 2007 Tournament; 20 countries competed at the Final stages; attendance figures topped two million for the first time; the Tournament was broadcast in 238 territories around the world; and by the time South Africa defeated England in the Final (watched by 17 million in the UK alone), the contest had been deemed the greatest Rugby World Cup of all time. No sooner had the dust settled, however, than attention shifted to the 2011 edition of the Tournament.

Bidding for the right to stage the Tournament had begun in 2005 with three countries: Japan, New Zealand and South Africa. Of the nominees, Japan were widely expected to win the vote: the country had an established infrastructure (it had successfully co-hosted the 2002 FIFA World Cup with South Korea) and many thought the time was right to take Rugby's showpiece into Asia for the first time. However, on 17 November 2005 in Dublin, it was announced that New Zealand had won the vote, despite the fact that, controversially, Oceania neighbours Australia had voted against them.

It was a huge coup for New Zealand Rugby. The country's ability to host an event of such stature had been brought into question: following the 1987 Tournament, many questioned the country's geographical isolation, the lack of accommodation for visitors and the paucity of stadiums. The country's cause was further hampered when, after being chosen to co-host the 2003 Tournament with Australia, it was dropped following a disagreement over ground-signage rights. Voices in some quarters suggested that New Zealand would never host a Rugby World Cup again. However, by the time Rugby World Cup 2011 kicks off at Eden Park in Auckland on 9 September 2011, such concerns are sure to be a distant memory: many of the grounds have been restructured, new ones have been built and the world will bear witness to the fact that no country has a greater passion for the Game. The seventh edition of Rugby World Cup could not have found a better home.

KNOW THE GAME

POOL PHASE

The Tournament's 20 nations have been drawn into four pools of five teams. Each team will play the other team in its pool on a round-robin basis. Four points will be awarded for a win, two for a draw and one for a defeat. After the completion of the ten pool matches, the top two teams will progress to the quarter-finals as the pool winner and the pool runner-up. If two teams finish the pool stage level on points, the higher-ranked team will be determined in the following way:

(i) the winner of the match between the two tied teams will be ranked higher;
(ii) if still level, the team with the higher points difference between points scored and points conceded will be ranked higher;
(iii) if still level, the team with the best difference between tries scored and tries conceded will be ranked higher;
(iv) if still level, the team that has scored the higher number of points in the pool stages will be ranked higher;
(v) if still level, the side that has scored the greater number of tries in the pool stages will be ranked higher;
(vi) if still level, the team with the higher ranking in the official IRB world rankings on the 1 September 2011 will be ranked higher.

KNOCKOUT MATCHES
Quarter-finals

The top two teams from each group will progress to the last eight and the quarter-final line-ups will be determined in the following way:

QF1: Winner Pool C v Runner-up Pool D   QF3: Winner Pool D v Runner-up Pool C
QF2: Winner Pool B v Runner-up Pool A   QF4: Winner Pool A v Runner-up Pool B

If the teams are tied at full-time, the winner will be decided in the following way:

(i) following a break of five minutes, a period of extra-time will follow, consisting of two periods of ten minutes with a five-minute interval in between;
(ii) if the teams are still tied, they will enter a period of sudden death in which the first team to score a point will be deemed the winner;
(iii) if the period of sudden death has not resulted in a winner, the teams will take part in a kicking competition, the winner of which will be declared the winner of the match.

The winners of the quarter-finals will progress to the semi-finals.

Semi-finals

The semi-final line-ups will be decided in the following manner:

SF1: Winner QF1 v Winner QF2   SF2: Winner QF3 v Winner QF4

In the event of a match ending in a tie following normal time, the same criteria used for the quarter-finals will be used to determine the winner. The winners will progress to the Final; the losers will progress to the Bronze Final.

Bronze Final

This match will be contested between the two losing semi-finalists. In the event of the match ending in a tie following normal time, the same criteria used for the quarter-finals will be used to determine the winner.

The Final

This match will be contested between the two winning semi-finalists. In the event of the match ending in a tie following normal time, the same criteria used for the quarter-finals will be used to determine the winner.

Made For Rugby: All Black History

International Rugby's all-time leading points-scorers (with 12,112 points in 472 matches – an impressive 25.7 points per match) and currently the only side to have a winning record against every team they have played, New Zealand, despite their relative failures in Rugby World Cup (they have won the game's biggest prize only once in six attempts), have established a deserved reputation as being the strongest Rugby nation on the planet.

Rugby has been played in New Zealand since the 1870s (England-educated Charles John Munroe is the man credited with bringing the game to the country), and although three decades would pass before New Zealand made their official debut on the international stage – a 22–3 victory over Australia in Sydney on 15 August 1903 – it did not take them long to establish a reputation as being a formidable opponent.

In 1905–06, a New Zealand team that came to be known as 'The Originals' – and who became the first to be dubbed the 'All Blacks' – toured Britain, France and Ireland and lost only one of their 32 matches, losing to Wales (0–3),

although controversy rages to this day over a disallowed New Zealand try that would have tied the scores at 3–3 and preserved the All Blacks unbeaten record. A team from Britain travelled to New Zealand in 1908 and lost the three-match series 2–0 (the second Test was drawn). New Zealand did not lose a match at home until 1913, a 5–16 defeat to Australia at Christchurch that was their only loss of the decade.

The 1920s saw the birth of one of the great rivalries of world Rugby: South Africa travelled to New Zealand for the first time and the closely contested three-match series ended in a 1–1 draw after the third test at Wellington

culminated in a 0–0 stalemate. In 1924–25, the All Blacks embarked on a 32-match tour to Britain, Ireland, France and Canada and went one better than The Originals by winning every single one of their matches – and duly earned the moniker 'The Invincibles'. In 1928, they contested their first-ever series on South African soil, which ended in a 2–2 draw after New Zealand won the fourth-and-final test in Cape Town to square the series. The 1920s ended on a downer, though, when they lost a three-test series in Australia 3–0.

The 1930s started with the British Lions first visit to the country, with the All Blacks rebounding from an opening-test defeat to win the series 3–1. Then, in Australia in 1932 and 1934, they finished level against the Wallabies. The battle against South Africa continued in 1937, with the Springboks winning a cracking three-match series in New Zealand 2–1. After the Second World War, Rugby in New Zealand resumed in 1946, and although the All Blacks started with four straight victories, they ended the decade with six straight defeats, including a second straight series defeat to South Africa.

All of which made South Africa's tour to New Zealand in 1956 one of the most eagerly anticipated series in history and the All Blacks' 3–1 victory represented not only their first-ever series victory over the Springboks, but also the point when the All Black legend started to grow. In 1959, they beat the Lions 3–1;

The All Blacks' pre-match *haka* has become part of Rugby folklore.

in 1963–64, only a 0–0 draw against Scotland prevented them from ending their tour to the United Kingdom with a Grand Slam; and between 1965 and 1970, New Zealand won all 17 of their matches – at the time, the longest winning streak in history.

In 1971, they lost 2–1 to the Lions (the All Blacks' only series defeat against the British tourists) following a 14–14 draw in the final test in Auckland. Two years later, they narrowly missed out on a Grand Slam over the four Home Nations after drawing 10–10 with Ireland in Dublin. Their decision to go ahead with their tour to South Africa in 1976 – after 33 African nations had withdrawn from the Olympic Games, held in Montreal earlier in the year, because of the International Olympic Committee's refusal to ban South Africa from the event (amid increasing global concern over the South African government's apartheid policy) – was a controversial one. It was a disappointing experience, too: they lost 3–1. It took a Grand Slam-winning tour of the United Kingdom and Ireland in 1978 to lift the gloom.

If the 1970s had been a decade of topsy-turvy results, then the 1980s was one of greater consistency. The unwanted malodour of tours (official and unofficial) to and from South Africa may have hung heavy over New Zealand for the best part of the decade, but the All Blacks' record during that period was impressive: they won 45 and drew three of their 57 matches and suffered only nine defeats. During that period they became the first team in history to lift the Rugby World Cup. It was the perfect fit: the best team in the world (particularly with South Africa languishing in sporting isolation) had collected the game's greatest prize. If New Zealand's Rugby story had stopped there, it would have been the perfect ending.

But, in Rugby World Cup terms at least, that was as good as it got for New Zealand. Unparalleled success may have continued to come their way in other areas of the game – they have won ten out of 15 Tri-Nations titles, continue to hold the upper hand over the British & Irish Lions and have stood on the top

of the IRB World Rankings longer than any other team in history – but, since 1987, the All Blacks have only appeared in one further Rugby World Cup Final (a defeat to South Africa, of all teams, in 1995) and have developed a tag as being the Tournament's perennial chokers. Reputation is everything to New Zealand Rugby and only victory at Rugby World Cup 2011 will remove this unwanted blemish on what has otherwise been an extraordinary Rugby history.

NEW ZEALAND RUGBY RECORDS

OVERALL PLAYING RECORD

Played:	472
Won:	354
Lost:	101
Drawn:	17
Points for:	12,112
Points against:	5,978

HONOURS

Rugby World Cup: World Champions (1987)

Tri-Nations: 1996, 1997, 1999, 2002, 2003, 2005, 2006, 2007, 2008, 2010

Biggest victory: 145–17 v Japan at Bloemfontein on 4 June 1995

Biggest defeat: 7–28 v Australia at Sydney on 28 August 1999

Longest-serving captain: Richie McCaw – 50 wins in 57 matches as captain between 2004 and 2010

LEADING POINTS-SCORERS: TOP FIVE

Pos	Points	Player (span)
1	1,188	Dan Carter (2003–10)
2	967	Andrew Mehrtens (1995–2004)
3	645	Grant Fox (1985–93)
4	291	Carlos Spencer (1997–2004)
5	245	Doug Howlett (2000–07)

LEADING TRY-SCORERS: TOP FIVE

Pos	Tries	Player (span)
1	49	Doug Howlett (2000–07)
2=	46	Christian Cullen (1996–2002)
=	46	Joe Rokocoko (2003–10)
4	44	Jeff Wilson (1993–2001)
5	37	Jonah Lomu (1994–2002)

MOST APPEARANCES: TOP FIVE

Pos	Caps	Player (span)
1=	94	Richie McCaw (2001–10)
=	94	Mils Muliaina (2003–10)
3	92	Sean Fitzpatrick (1986–1997)
4	83	Keven Mealamu (2002–10)
5	81	Justin Marshall (1995–2005)

Can Richie McCaw be New Zealand's new captain fantastic and lead them to glory in 2011?

Greats Of New Zealand Rugby

Given their status as the most successful country in international Rugby, any list of the game's all-time great players will invariably feature a host of New Zealand players. Coming up with a list of the top-five All Blacks is an almost impossible task; instead, here are the five players who have arguably had the biggest impact on New Zealand Rugby.

* GfM = Goals from Mark. Until September 1977, a player could catch a high ball, call mark and take a shot at goal (from the point where the mark was called) for three points.

DON CLARKE

Born: ..10 November 1933, Pihama, New Zealand
Position: ....Full-back
Caps: 31
Points: 207 (2t, 33c, 38p, 5dg, 2GfM*)
Debut: .... v South Africa at Christchurch
....on 18 August 1956
Last game: ....v Australia at Wellington
....on 29 August 1964

Renowned for his exceptional kicking abilities (he was nicknamed 'The Boot'), Don Clarke was an imposing full-back who made his first appearance for Waikato aged 17, but shot to prominence in 1956 when he played a leading role in a 14–10 victory over the touring Springboks. He made his international debut against South Africa in the third test of their tour in Christchurch (he scored two penalties and a conversion in a 17–10 victory). He was the All Blacks' hero in the first test against the 1959 British Lions, kicking a then-world-record six penalties to help his side to a slender 18–17 victory, and again proved his status not only as a match-winner but also as a kicker of the highest calibre against France at Wellington in 1961, when he slotted a touchline conversion in gale-force conditions in New Zealand's 5–3 victory. Clarke went on to play in 31 tests for his country (losing only four) until a serious knee injury in 1964 brought his distinguished career to a close. He died in 2002.

COLIN MEADS

Born: ..... 3 June 1936, Cambridge, New Zealand
Position: ....Flanker/lock/No. 8
Caps: 55
Points: 21 (7t)
Debut: .... v Australia at Sydney
.... on 25 May 1957
Last game: ....v British Lions at Auckland
....on 14 August 1971

A supreme competitor in the lineout (hence his nickname, 'Pinetree'), Colin Meads was also a fearsome ball carrier considered by many to have been the best of his generation. He made his international debut in the first test of New Zealand's tour to Australia in 1957 and scored his first international try (of seven) in the second test – having played both matches at flanker. He played at lock against the Wallabies in 1958 and switched between the two positions, before settling on lock. There was an air of indestructibility about Meads: on his first tour to South Africa in 1960, aged 24, he played in 20 of the All Blacks' 26 games – a colossal amount given the high standard of Rugby; back in South Africa a decade later, he fractured his forearm in a match against Eastern Transvaal but returned to action five weeks later to play a full part in the tour. But even Meads could not go on forever: his 55-test career spanning three decades came to an end after New Zealand's series defeat to the Lions in 1971.

WAYNE SHELFORD

Born: .... 13 December 1957, Rotorua,
.... New Zealand
Position: ....No. 8
Caps: 22
Points: 20 (5t)
Debut: ....v France at Toulouse
...................................on 8 November 1986
Last game: .... v Scotland at Auckland
..................................on 23 June 1990

A player of no-nonsense commitment and aggression with an indomitable will to win, Wayne 'Buck' Shelford had a relatively brief career, but his name is writ large in New Zealand Rugby. Having waited in the shadows of No. 8 great Murray Mexted, Shelford made his debut, aged 28, against France in 1986. He played in New Zealand's Rugby World Cup-winning team a year later and became captain in 1988. His reputation was forged as one of the game's hard men – he played on in a match against France after his scrotum had been ripped in a scrum – and as an inspired captain (New Zealand won 13 and drew one of their 14 Test matches under his charge). So when coach Alex Wyllie dropped him in 1990 – and New Zealand's Rugby fortunes started to change – it did not take long before the 'Bring Back Buck' campaign started in earnest.

MICHAEL JONES

Born: ....8 April 1965, Auckland, New Zealand
Position: ....Flanker
Caps: 55
Points: 56 (13t)
Debut: ....(for New Zealand) v Italy
.... at Auckland on 22 May 1987
Last game: .... v Australia at Christchurch
...................................on 1 August 1998

With his pace, strength, ball-handling skills and aggressive defence, it was clear from his early days that Michael Jones was destined for stardom and, although he had played in one test for Western Samoa (against Wales in June 1986), he was selected for New Zealand's Rugby World Cup 1987 squad. After a serious knee injury in 1989 he was selected for Rugby World Cup 1991, and seemed to have lost none of his edge when scoring New Zealand's first try in their opening-game victory over England. However, staunch religious beliefs (he would not play on Sundays) saw him miss three matches during the Tournament and for that reason, he wasn't selected to play in 1995. He switched to blindside in the mid-1990s and, in 1996, helped New Zealand to both the inaugural Tri-Nations title and a first series win in South Africa, but by 1998, aged 33, it was clear that time and injuries had caught up with him. His final game for New Zealand was against Australia on 1 August 1998.

JONAH LOMU

Born: ....12 May 1975, Auckland, New Zealand
Position: ....Wing
Caps: 63
Points: 185 (37t)
Debut: .... v France at Christchurch
...................................on 26 June 1994
Last game: .... v Wales at Millennium Stadium
....on 23 November 2002

The most destructive player in history, the world only ever saw the best of Jonah Lomu at Rugby World Cup 1995 and 1999; in between, the giant winger faced a constant fight against injury and illness. Ironically, given the impact he made on the Tournament, Lomu almost missed out on Rugby World Cup 1995. Having become the youngest-ever All Black in June 1994 (aged 19 years 45 days), he failed numerous fitness tests and was considered a gamble when selected. He proved unstoppable, scoring seven tries and ending the Tournament as the most talked-about player on the planet. After post-Tournament health problems, he was back to his best at Rugby World Cup 1999, scoring a Tournament-record eight tries. He was one of the few All Blacks to emerge from a disastrous campaign with his reputation enhanced. As the effects of his kidney condition kicked in, however, the magic started to fade and by 2003 he had disappeared from the international scene.

Match Venues

As part of the philosophy of New Zealand's winning bid – that Rugby World Cup 2011 should be contested in a 'Stadium of Four Million' (so ran the slogan) – 12 venues across the country will host matches during the Tournament, nine of them in the North Island and three in the South. All of the competition's concluding matches will be played at Eden Park in Auckland.

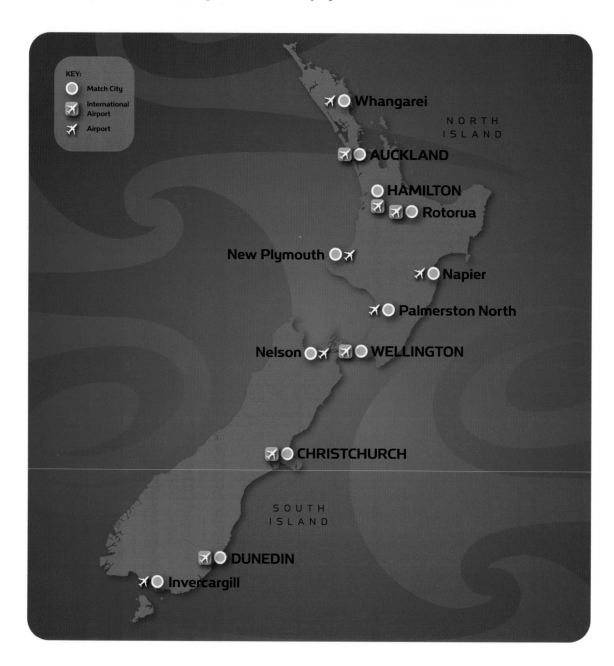

KEY:

○ Match City

✈ International Airport

✈ Airport

Whangarei

NORTH ISLAND

AUCKLAND

HAMILTON

Rotorua

New Plymouth

Napier

Palmerston North

Nelson

WELLINGTON

CHRISTCHURCH

SOUTH ISLAND

DUNEDIN

Invercargill

EDEN PARK, AUCKLAND

Capacity: 60,000

Matches hosted:
New Zealand v Tonga (A, 9 Sept);
Australia v Ireland (C, 17 Sept);
New Zealand v France (A, 24 Sept);
Fiji v Samoa (D, 25 Sept);
England v Scotland (B, 1 Oct);
Quarter-final 2 (8 Oct);
Quarter-final 4 (9 Oct);
Semi-final 1 (15 Oct);
Semi-final 2 (16 Oct);
Bronze Final (21 Oct);
Rugby World Cup Final 2011 (23 Oct)

The largest and most revered stadium in the country and the venue for the Final of Rugby World Cup 1987, Eden Park, located less than 3km (2 miles) away from Auckland's business district, has been a fortress for New Zealand Rugby in recent years (the All Blacks last lost there against France on 3 July 1994 and have won 21 and drawn one of their 22 matches at the venue since). Expanded to increase the capacity to 60,000, the ground will host 11 games, including the Rugby World Cup Final.

Eden Park, Auckland, will be the proud host of the Rugby World Cup 2011 Final.

NORTH HARBOUR STADIUM, AUCKLAND

Capacity: 30,000

Matches hosted:
France v Japan (A, 10 Sept);
South Africa v Namibia (D, 22 Sept);
South Africa v Samoa (D, 30 Sept)

Located in the centre of Albany, 19km (12 miles) from Auckland, North Harbour Stadium is a modern-built, all-purpose stadium that was opened in 1997. It is home to the North Harbour club, who compete in New Zealand provincial Rugby, and will host three matches at Rugby World Cup 2011.

Stadium Christchurch has a history of hosting matches that dates back to 1880.

STADIUM CHRISTCHURCH, CHRISTCHURCH

Capacity: 44,000

At the time of going to press, these matches are to be relocated, see rugbyworldcup.com for updates:
Argentina v England (B, 10 Sept);
Australia v Italy (C, 11 Sept);
England v Georgia (B, 18 Sept);
Argentina v Scotland (B, 25 Sept);
Australia v Russia (C, 1 Oct);

Situated in the centre of Christchurch, New Zealand's second largest city, Stadium Christchurch has hosted Rugby matches since 1880, when it was opened as Lancaster Park. It went on to provide the setting for some memorable international matches, both in Rugby and cricket, and, in 2009, underwent a major upgrade for Rugby World Cup 2011, before the devastating earthquake of 22 February 2011 ended its viability as a host venue.

OTAGO STADIUM, DUNEDIN

Capacity: 30,000
Matches hosted:
Scotland v Georgia (B, 14 Sept);
England v Romania (B, 24 Sept);
Ireland v Italy (C, 2 Oct)

Built at a cost of NZ$200 million and due to open in August 2011, the Otago Stadium, a 40-minute drive from Dunedin airport in New Zealand's South Island, is a state-of-the-art facility that features an all-weather transparent permanent roof and a natural turf playing surface – making it the world's first fully enclosed grass stadium. It will host three matches during Rugby World Cup 2011.

McLean Park on North Island is an already well-known international sports stadium.

WAIKATO STADIUM, HAMILTON

Capacity: 30,000
Matches hosted:
New Zealand v Japan (A, 16 Sept);
Wales v Samoa (D, 18 Sept);
Wales v Fiji (D, 2 Oct)

Located in Hamilton, on the banks of the Waikato River in the centre of the North Island, Waikato Stadium has been the home of Waikato Rugby since 1925 and of international Rugby since 1987. The redeveloped stadium was opened in 2002 and has cemented a reputation as a world-class venue.

RUGBY PARK STADIUM, INVERCARGILL

Capacity: 17,000
Matches hosted:
Scotland v Romania (B, 10 Sept);
Argentina v Romania (B, 17 Sept)

Rugby Park Stadium in Invercargill – sitting on the tip of the South Island it is the southernmost of Rugby World Cup 2011's 13 venues – was established in 1990 as the home of the Southland provincial Rugby team, although the ground itself has existed since 1923. It was redeveloped in 2001, and will play host to two matches.

McLEAN PARK, NAPIER

Capacity: 15,000
Matches hosted:
France v Canada (A, 18 Sept);
Canada v Japan (A, 27 Sept)

McLean Park in Napier, the art deco city on New Zealand's east coast, is an established home for international sport, particularly cricket, where it has hosted international matches since 1979. The All Blacks have played one fixture at the venue: a 51–10 victory over Samoa on 7 June 1996.

TRAFALGAR PARK, NELSON

Capacity: 18,000
Matches hosted:
Italy v Russia (C, 20 Sept);
Italy v USA (C, 27 Sept)

Trafalgar Park in Nelson – the so-called sunshine city of New Zealand on the northern tip of the South Island – is one of the home grounds for New Zealand domestic club Tasman and for the Central Districts regional cricket side. The stadium has been expanded for Rugby World Cup 2011 and it will host two matches at the Tournament.

Waikato Stadium was redeveloped in 2002 to become a world-class Rugby venue.

Stadium Taranaki is named after the spectacular mountain that forms a backdrop to the area.

WELLINGTON REGIONAL STADIUM, WELLINGTON

Capacity: 40,000
Matches hosted:
South Africa v Wales (D, 11 Sept);
South Africa v Fiji (D, 17 Sept);
Australia v USA (C, 23 Sept);
France v Tonga (A, 1 Oct);
New Zealand v Canada (A, 2 Oct);
Quarter-final 1 (8 Oct);
Quarter-final 3 (9 Oct)

Wellington Regional Stadium in New Zealand's capital city, Wellington, was built on the old railway yards close to the city centre, opened in 2000 and has hosted football, Rugby and cricket internationals. Known colloquially as 'The Cake Tin', due to its shape and silver-coloured outer walls, it will host seven matches at Rugby World Cup 2011 (only Auckland's Eden Park will host more), including two of the quarter-finals.

STADIUM TARANAKI, NEW PLYMOUTH

Capacity: 26,000
Matches hosted:
Ireland v USA (C, 11 Sept);
Russia v USA (C, 15 Sept);
Wales v Namibia (D, 26 Sept)

Situated in New Plymouth, a modern coastal city set against the stunning backdrop of Mount Taranaki, Stadium Taranaki (formerly known as the Yarrow Stadium) is the Taranaki region's home of Rugby with a history dating back to 1931. The stadium underwent significant modernization in 2002 and will host three matches at Rugby World Cup 2011. In May 2009 it was named as the third best stadium on earth by *New Zealand Rugby World* magazine.

ARENA MANAWATU, PALMERSTON NORTH

Capacity: 15,000
Matches hosted:
Georgia v Romania (B, 28 Sept);
Argentina v Georgia (B, 2 Oct)

Located in Palmerston North, halfway between Lake Taupo in the centre of the New Zealand's North Island and the country's capital Wellington in the extreme south, Arena Manawatu, the sometime home of the Wellington Hurricanes, holds the distinction of having hosted the first-ever Super 12 (against Auckland Blues in 1996).

ROTORUA INTERNATIONAL STADIUM, ROTORUA

Capacity: 26,000
Matches hosted:
Fiji v Namibia (D, 10 Sept);
Samoa v Namibia (D, 14 Sept);
Ireland v Russia (C, 25 Sept)

Originally built in 1911 but renovated several times since, the Rotorua International Stadium, located in the world-famous thermal-spa city, is one of the two home grounds for Bay of Plenty Rugby Union. Wales fans will remember it well: the stadium hosted the bronze-medal match at the inaugural Rugby World Cup 1987, when Paul Thorburn's last-gasp touchline conversion handed the Welsh a memorable 22–21 victory over a powerful Australia side.

NORTHLAND EVENTS CENTRE, WHANGEREI

Capacity: 18,000
Matches hosted:
Tonga v Canada (A, 14 Sept);
Tonga v Japan (A, 21 Sept)

The most northerly of the 13 venues, the Northland Events Centre in Whangarei is the traditional home of Northland Rugby and has hosted several memorable international matches over the years. The stadium underwent a major upgrade (completed in 2011) in preparation for Rugby World Cup 2011.

Rotorua has already hosted a Rugby World Cup match, in 1987.

Tourist Highlights: North Island

The most populous of New Zealand's two main islands (it contains 75 per cent of the country's population), the North Island is home to both New Zealand's capital city, Wellington, and its largest, Auckland. Renowned for volcanic activity, such as the hot mud pools and geysers in Rotorua, it is an island of diversity: temperate in the south and tropical in the north.

AUCKLAND

The largest, most populous (with 1.3 million people) and most cosmopolitan of New Zealand's cities, Auckland was originally inhabited by Maori people, who called it 'Tamaki Makau Rau' – meaning 'a maiden with 100 lovers'. The city is situated on an isthmus (2km/1.25 miles wide at its narrowest) and is nicknamed the 'City of the Sails' because it has more yachts per capita than any other city in the world. But there is far more to Auckland than sea and sails: the city boasts museums, art galleries, a zoo, the most vibrant nightlife in New Zealand and some of the country's finest restaurants.

BAY OF ISLANDS

Situated in the Northland region of New Zealand, the Bay of Islands – a 16km/10-mile-wide inlet containing more than 150 islands – is richly infused with both Maori and European history (it was the first area in the country to be settled by Europeans). One of the most popular sailing and fishing destinations in the country, its white-sand beaches, natural beauty and tempting blue waters make it both an ideal aquatic playground or the perfect place for a peaceful retreat. In a survey in 2006, the area was found to have the second-bluest skies in the world (after Rio de Janeiro in Brazil).

COROMANDEL PENINSULA

Lying 55km (35 miles) to the east of Auckland on the other side of Hauraki Gulf, the rustic, relaxed and unspoilt Coromandel Peninsula is a favourite holiday destination for New Zealanders. It is an area of outstanding natural beauty, with rugged volcanic hills cloaked in native rainforest and over 400km (250 miles) of spectacular coastline where the white-sanded beach of your dreams is only ever just around the next corner. Famed for yachting and scuba-diving, the area's other attractions include visiting abandoned gold mines or digging your own mud pool at Hot Water Beach on the east of the peninsula.

Auckland: New Zealand's biggest and most cosmopolitan city.

Bay of Islands: a Mecca for watersports and the perfect place for a restful retreat.

ROTORUA

Set on the edge of a large lake, in the centre of what was once a volcano, in an area of continued geothermic activity, Rotorua's mud pools, geysers (notably the Pohutu Geyser near Whakarewarewa village), hot thermal springs and buried village have made it the tourist capital of New Zealand. Nicknamed the 'Sulphur City' because of the sulphurous odour that continually hangs over the area, the city is also the centre of Maori culture: they were the first settlers in the region (over 200 years ago) and the area's subterranean activity lies at the very heart of many Maori legends.

TONGARIRO NATIONAL PARK

New Zealand's oldest national park (established in 1887 it is the fourth oldest in the world) and also a World Heritage site (recognizing its importance to Maori culture as well as its spectacular volcanic landscape), Tongariro National Park lies at the heart of New Zealand's North Island – 330km (205 miles) south of Auckland and 320km (200 miles) north of Wellington. Particular highlights in the area include alpine trekking over varied volcanic terrain, climbing to the crater's edge of the Mount Ruapehu volcano, game fishing, horse riding and white-water rafting. The area is also a popular skiing destination in the winter.

Rotorua: the hot mud pools and geysers have been a magnet for tourists since the 19th century.

Tourist Highlights: South Island

The larger of New Zealand's two main islands, the South Island is a wild and wonderful paradise of towering snow-capped peaks, waterfalls that cascade into sleepy fjords and glaciers melting into serene lakes. But it's not all wilderness: there are adventure holidays, a city break in Christchurch or Dunedin or the produce of the world's most southerly vineyards.

Fiordland National Park: all the drama and beauty of New Zealand's amazing scenery packed into one remote wilderness.

ABEL TASMAN NATIONAL PARK

Named after Dutch explorer Abel Tasman who, in 1642, became the first European explorer to sight New Zealand, this is the smallest of the country's national parks, measuring just 225 sq. km (87 sq. miles), and is located on the northwestern tip of the South Island. It is the perfect getaway location, a place where lazy days on one of the area's renowned golden beaches can be offset by kayaking or sailing in crystal-clear deep blue water or freshwater inlets, or trekking along one of the park's many tracks, either along the impressive granite-cliff coastline or through the area's mountainous, forested interior.

FIORDLAND NATIONAL PARK

One of the most dramatic and beautiful parts of New Zealand, Fiordland National Park, a vast, remote wilderness, renowned as being the home of Milford and Doubtful Sounds and Mitre Peak (all carved out of the landscape by glaciers during successive ice ages) and for numerous breathtaking treks. Located in the southwest corner of the South Island, with much of the area inaccessible by road, it is the largest of New Zealand's 14 national parks – with an area of 12,120 sq. km (4,680 sq. miles) – and lies at the very heart of the Te Wahipounamu – South West New Zealand World Heritage area.

MOUNT COOK NATIONAL PARK

Mount Cook National Park (named after the country's highest mountain, which stands at 3,754m/12,316ft) is New Zealand's upper alpine region, containing sky-scraping peaks (19 of them over 3,000m/9,840ft), the longest glaciers in the country (the mighty Tasman Glacier is 27km/16.8 miles in length) and permanent snowfields, and holds the best mountaineering in the Australasian region (it was where a young Sir Edmund Hillary fine-tuned his technique before becoming the first person to conquer Mount Everest). Located in the heart of the Southern Alps in central South Island, the area was established as a national park in 1953.

QUEENSTOWN

Located in the southwest corner of New Zealand's South Island (a two-hour flight away from Auckland), deep in the Southern Alps on Lake Wakatipu, Queenstown is the country's premier alpine resort and a renowned centre for action-packed adventure holidays, with activities such as skydiving, bungee jumping, white-water rafting, skiing and jet-boating all readily available. For those with more sedate leanings, there are numerous trekking routes in the area or, as a real treat, helicopter rides through Lord of the Rings country. And that's only during the day: the town's varied nightlife will keep visitors entertained from dusk through till dawn.

WESTLAND NATIONAL PARK

Established as a national park in 1960 and containing more than 60 glaciers, with two of them – the fast-moving Fox and Franz Josef glaciers – the only glaciers in the world that flow down into temperate rainforest, Westland National Park is an exquisite slice of wilderness that extends from some of the highest peaks in the Southern Alps to the gentle rainforests on the rugged and remote coastline that borders the Tasman Sea. Located in the northwest of the South Island, the area, the stunning scenery apart, is a treasure trove of amazing geology, rare flora and fauna and wonderful history.

Queenstown: the action-adventure holiday capital of the world.

Westland National Park: New Zealand at its purest.

NEW ZEALAND WIN INAUGURAL TITLE
20 JUNE 1987, EDEN PARK, AUCKLAND

After years of planning, the first Rugby World Cup, co-hosted by Australia and New Zealand, finally kicked off in 1987. The International Rugby Board invited 16 teams from five continents to attend the Tournament to contest 32 matches and by the 32nd match only two teams were still standing: co-hosts New Zealand, who had eased into the Final looking stronger every match, and France, the reigning northern hemisphere champions and the competition's form team who had shocked pre-Tournament favourites Australia in the semi-finals with an exhilarating display of attacking never-say-die Rugby. Everyone was expecting a free-flowing game that would befit the occasion; instead it was an eerily one-sided affair. A subdued France struggled as New Zealand dominated the match from start to finish, outscoring France by three tries to one (from Michael Jones, David Kirk and John Kirwan) to win the match 29–9 and become Rugby's first World Champions.

Smiles all round as David Kirk becomes the first man in history to lift the Webb Ellis Cup.

THE ROAD TO NEW ZEALAND

On 17 November 2005, in Dublin, it was announced that New Zealand – who had based their bid around an unquestioned passion for the game, an immense contribution to its history over the years and a promise to put on a Tournament for Rugby people by Rugby people – had triumphed over Japan and South Africa for the right to host the biggest competition in the sport: Rugby World Cup 2011. Preparations for the Tournament off the field of play began immediately; on the field of play, qualification matches kicked off in March 2008, with a record total of 86 countries vying for eight available places, and it wasn't until December 2010 that the final line-up for the Tournament was known.

Japan beat Hong Kong in their 2010 Asian Five Nations match to qualify for Rugby World Cup 2011.

How The Bid Was Won

The bidding process for the right to host Rugby World Cup 2011 started as early as February 2005 when three countries – Japan, New Zealand and South Africa – formally submitted their bids. After weeks of canvassing support, the results were announced in Dublin on 17 November and the world was in for a surprise: the bookmakers may not have fancied their chances, but New Zealand had won the right to host Rugby World Cup 2011.

Japan were the early favourites to win the bid and the reasons for that status were compelling: victory would have seen the Tournament contested in Asia for the first time, thus fulfilling the International Rugby Board's long-held dream of using the event as a vehicle for spreading the game's gospel to the furthest reaches of the globe. Also, having successfully co-hosted the 2002 FIFA World Cup (with South Korea), the infrastructure required to stage such a competition was already in place and with the country's vast economic wealth it was clear that no expense would be spared if it came to both staging and marketing it.

Next on the bookmakers' lists were South Africa, whose bid was led by iconic former captain François Pienaar,

the man who had lifted the Trophy for the Springboks the last time the Tournament had been staged in the country in 1995. The focal point of South Africa's bid was that, having hosted the 2010 FIFA World Cup only a year before the Tournament was due to be staged, the world-class infrastructure was already in place.

Propping up the trio, in the bookies eyes at least, was New Zealand, the co-hosts of the inaugural event in 1987, who had been expected to co-host the 2003 event only to withdraw after a disagreement over ground-signage rights. Their bid was not without its critics. From a geographical point of view, the time difference made it a harder sell to wealthy European broadcasters, it was far from the easiest venue for the fans to get to and, once

they were there, questions were raised as to whether the general infrastructure could cope with them.

The huge success of the 2005 British & Irish Lions tour, which saw fans descend on the country in their thousands only months before the decision as to who would host Rugby World Cup 2011 was to be made, silenced those doubters, however, and instead of concentrating on commercialism and strategic advantage (both economic and geographic), the New Zealand bid focused on the impact they had made on the world game over the years and the unbridled passion the country had developed for it. There was another, more pragmatic, reason behind New Zealand's government-backed bid: the general consensus in and around the national Rugby union at the time was that if they didn't bid then, there was a likelihood that the Tournament – which had already mushroomed into the third largest sporting event on the planet (behind the Olympic Games and the FIFA World Cup) – would simply, and naturally, outgrow the country.

With the result of the process due to be announced in Dublin on 17 November 2005, the final bid presentations brought in the heavyweights, with New Zealand, in particular, calling in the big guns, notably prime minister Helen Clarke, former All Black legend Colin Meads and the then-current captain of the national team Tana Umaga.

In the first round of voting, when the three bidding countries were not allowed to take part, there were 19 votes available but, in accordance with

The ultimate prize: 20 teams will fight for the right to lift the Webb Ellis Cup.

IRB rules and regulations, 12 of those votes were held by just six countries – Australia, England, France, Ireland, Scotland and Wales. Argentina, Canada and Italy held one vote each, while the final vote was shared between the confederations of Africa, Asia, the Americas, Europe and Oceania.

Surprisingly, South Africa fell at the first voting hurdle and their fall changed the odds dramatically. Having been eliminated from the bidding process, the South Africans (who held two votes) announced that they were backing New Zealand's bid (allegedly because of the support the country had shown towards the anti-apartheid movement during the Springboks 1981 tour to New Zealand). The announcement seemed to swing the odds in New Zealand's favour, although many still expected the sheer scale of Japan's economic weight to redress the balance … the wait was agonizing. In the end, however, it was New Zealand's emotional appeal that won the day and Rugby World Cup 2011 could not have found a more suitable home.

Global appeal: a giant ball promoting Rugby World Cup 2011 is lit up at Tokyo Tower, Japan.

NEW ZEALAND'S WINNING BID PLEDGES

1. A TOURNAMENT FOR THE PLAYERS

An environment where players can perform at their very best

Rugby facilities that are excellent and close at hand

A Tournament based on traditional Rugby values

2. A TOURNAMENT FOR VISITING FANS

A country that will be welcoming and safe

3. A TOURNAMENT FOR FANS AT HOME

Superb broadcast coverage

4. A COMMERCIALLY SUCCESSFUL TOURNAMENT

Unique partnership between Rugby and government

Tournament fee guaranteed

Conservative budget – delivering most commercially successful Rugby World Cup ever

Tournament clean stadia requirements met

5. A SHOWCASE EVENT

A Tournament that runs smoothly and seamlessly

A Tournament that will be media-friendly

Stable country and national union

6. A TOURNAMENT FOR RUGBY EVERYWHERE

A safe option

Worthy guardians of Rugby's jewel in the crown

Global Rugby legacy

How The Teams Qualified

With the top three placed teams in the group stages at Rugby World Cup 2007 all gaining direct entry into the 2011 Tournament, it left 86 teams competing for the eight remaining places up for grabs. The battle to claim them got underway when St Vincent and the Grenadines played Mexico in Kingstown on 29 March 2008 and culminated 21 months later when Romania met Uruguay in Bucharest on 27 November 2010. Below is what happened in between.

AFRICA
(Namibia)

The 2008 Africa Cup served as Africa's Rugby World Cup 2011 qualifying Tournament. The initial phase consisted of four pools of three teams (each team played one match at home and one away) with the winners of each group – Namibia, Ivory Coast, Tunisia and Uganda – progressing to the semi-finals (which would be contested on a home-and-away basis). Namibia – Africa's only team to come through the qualifying rounds for the last three Rugby World Cups – saw off the Ivory Coast in the first of the last-four clashes (drawing 13–13 away and winning 51–14 at home) and it was a similar story for Tunisia in the second (they beat Uganda 41–17 away and 38–13 at home). The qualification Final was a closer affair, with Namibia earning hard-fought wins in Tunis (18–13) and Windhoek (22–10) to maintain their impressive recent qualifying record, while Tunisia progressed to the repechage round.

AMERICAS
(Canada, United States)

For the second successive campaign, the Americas section, although labelled under a single umbrella, was essentially two separate Tournaments that intertwined only rarely. The champions of North America took one automatic qualifying spot with the runners-up playing the winners of a lengthy qualifying process to decide the other with the loser of that match moving into the repechage round. Trinidad and Tobago came out on top of the nine-team struggle in the initial qualifying stage (round 1a), beating Guyana (40–24) in the final. The South American equivalent saw Brazil finish on top of a five-team group. Brazil then beat Trinidad and Tobago (31–8 away and 24–12 at home) to progress as regional champions. And then came the business end of the Tournament: Canada beat the United States 47–30 on aggregate to claim the first automatic qualifying spot and Uruguay won both of their matches in a three-team group (containing Brazil and Chile) to earn the right to play the United States for the one remaining place. The United States won both matches in the two-leg Final (27–22 away and 27–6 at home) to win a ticket to New Zealand, while Uruguay moved into the repechage round.

ASIA
(Japan)

After two early rounds to decide which five teams would make up the five-team league, Asia's Rugby World Cup 2011 qualifying campaign (with one automatic qualifying place available) was ultimately decided by the final standings in the 2010 Asian Five Nations Championship. There were few surprises when it came to the winner – Japan won all four of their matches with ease (scoring a total of 326 points and conceding a mere 30) to maintain their proud record of having qualified for every Rugby World Cup – but the squabble for second (and a place in the repechage round) threw up a shock or two. South Korea, perennial bridesmaids in Asian Rugby to Japan in recent years, lost all four of their matches to finish fifth and after the remaining three teams – Arabian Gulf,

The USA and Canada lock horns during qualifying for Rugby World Cup 2011.

Georgia earn their place in 2011.

of playoff matches to earn the right to progress to the repechage. Georgia were the Tournament's form team, winning eight and drawing one of their ten matches to secure a place at Rugby World Cup 2011 for the third successive time. The second qualification spot went to Russia, who won seven and drew one of their matches to win a place on the game's greatest stage for the first time. Third-placed Romania kept their hopes of maintaining their 100 per cent appearance record in the Tournament by beating Ukraine (94–10 on aggregate) in the last of the playoffs to move into the repechage.

Hong Kong and Kazakhstan – recorded identical records (won two, lost two), it was Kazakhstan who progressed by dint of having scored the most tries.

EUROPE (Georgia, Russia)

The 2008–10 European Nations Cup (also known as the Six Nations B Championship) served as the initial stages of Europe's Rugby World Cup 2011 qualifying Tournament, with the top two teams gaining automatic qualification and the third-placed team moving into the final round of a series

OCEANIA (Samoa)

With Fiji and Tonga qualifying automatically for Rugby World Cup 2011 as a result of their performances at RWC 2007, it came as little surprise when Samoa claimed Oceania's one available qualifying spot by thumping Papua New Guinea (who had emerged as winners of an initial four-team qualifying phase) 188–19 on aggregate.

REPECHAGE ROUND (Romania)

Only four teams – Kazakhstan, Romania, Tunisia and Uruguay – remained in

the battle for Rugby World Cup 2011's final qualifying spot. In the first of the semi-finals (one-off affairs, with home advantage given to the team with the higher IRB World Ranking), Romania beat Tunisia (56–13); Uruguay beat Kazakhstan (44–17) in the second. Romania then gained the upper hand in the two-leg final when they battled to a 21–21 draw in Montevideo and completed their 15-match campaign on a high when they won the return leg in Bucharest 39–12 – they were on their way to New Zealand.

Romania's final repechage victory.

RUGBY WORLD CUP 2011 QUALIFYING: AT A GLANCE

THE QUALIFIERS

Africa: ....Namibia
Americas: .... Canada, United States
Asia: ....Japan
Europe: .... Georgia, Russia
Oceania: ....Samoa
Repechage: ....Romania

LEADING POINTS-SCORERS: TOP FIVE

Pos	Points	Player (country)
1	105	Yuriy Kushnarev (Rus)
2	94	Dan Dumbrava (Rom)
3	82	Shaun Webb (Jap)
4	80	Merab Kvirikashvili (Geo)
5	68	Pedro Cabral (Por)

LEADING TRY-SCORERS: TOP FIVE

Pos	Tries	Player (country)
1	8	Kosuke Endo (Jap)
=	8	Catalin Fercu (Rom)
3=	7	Stefan Ciuntu (Rom)
=	7	Alexander Gvozdovsky (Rus)
=	7	Takashi Kikutani (Jap)
=	7	Alisi Tupuailei (Jap)
=	7	Adam Raby (HK)

BIGGEST VICTORIES: TOP FIVE

Pos	Score	Winner	Opponent	Venue	Date
1	115–7	Samoa	Papua New Guinea	Apia	11 Jul 2009
2	101–7	Japan	Kazakhstan	Tokyo	15 May 2010
3	94–5	Japan	Hong Kong	Tokyo	22 May 2010
4	87–10	Japan	Kazakhstan	Tokyo	25 Apr 2009
5	79–3	Chile	Brazil	Vina del Mar	25 Apr 2009

POOL A

9 September	20:30	Eden Park, Auckland
New Zealand		**Tonga**

10 September	18:00	North Harbour, Auckland
France		**Japan**

14 September	17:00	Whangarei
Tonga		**Canada**

16 September	20:00	Hamilton
New Zealand		**Japan**

18 September	20:30	Napier
France		**Canada**

21 September	19:30	Whangarei
Tonga		**Japan**

24 September	20:30	Eden Park, Auckland
New Zealand		**France**

27 September	17:00	Napier
Canada		**Japan**

1 October	18:00	Wellington
France		**Tonga**

2 October	15:30	Wellington
New Zealand		**Canada**

FINAL POOL A TABLE

Pos	Team	P	W	L	D	PF	PA	Pts
A1								
A2								
A3								
A4								
A5								

POOL B

10 September	13:00	Invercargill
Scotland		**Romania**

10 September	20:30	see rugbyworldcup.com
Argentina		**England**

14 September	19:30	Dunedin
Scotland		**Georgia**

17 September	15:30	Invercargill
Argentina		**Romania**

18 September	18:00	see rugbyworldcup.com
England		**Georgia**

24 September	18:00	Dunedin
England		**Romania**

25 September	20:30	see rugbyworldcup.com
Argentina		**Scotland**

28 September	19:30	Palmerston North
Georgia		**Romania**

1 October	20:30	Eden Park, Auckland
England		**Scotland**

2 October	13:00	Palmerston North
Argentina		**Georgia**

FINAL POOL B TABLE

Pos	Team	P	W	L	D	PF	PA	Pts
B1								
B2								
B3								
B4								
B5								

QUARTER-FINALS

QF1 8 October	18:00	Wellington
C1		D2

QF2 8 October	20:30	Eden Park, Auckland
B1		A2

QF3 9 October	18:00	Wellington
D1		C2

QF4 9 October	20:30	Eden Park, Auckland
A1		B2

SEMI-FINALS

SF1 15 October	21:00	Eden Park, Auckland
Winner QF1		Winner QF2

SF2 16 October	21:00	Eden Park, Auckland
Winner QF3		Winner QF4

BRONZE FINAL

BRONZE FINAL 21 October	20:30	Eden Park, Auckland
Runner-up SF1		Runner-up SF2

POOL C

11 September	15:30	see rugbyworldcup.com
Australia		**Italy**

11 September	18:00	New Plymouth
Ireland		**USA**

15 September	19:30	New Plymouth
Russia		**USA**

17 September	20:30	Auckland
Australia		**Ireland**

20 September	19:30	Nelson
Italy		**Russia**

23 September	20:30	Wellington
Australia		**USA**

25 September	18:00	Rotorua
Ireland		**Russia**

27 September	19:30	Nelson
Italy		**USA**

1 October	15:30	see rugbyworldcup.com
Australia		**Russia**

2 October	20:30	Dunedin
Ireland		**Italy**

FINAL POOL C TABLE

Pos	Team	P	W	L	D	PF	PA	Pts
C1								
C2								
C3								
C4								
C5								

POOL D

10 September	15:30	Rotorua
Fiji		**Namibia**

11 September	20:30	Wellington
South Africa		**Wales**

14 September	14:30	Rotorua
Samoa		**Namibia**

17 September	18:00	Wellington
South Africa		**Fiji**

18 September	15:30	Hamilton
Wales		**Samoa**

22 September	20:00	North Harbour, Auckland
South Africa		**Namibia**

25 September	15:30	Eden Park, Auckland
Fiji		**Samoa**

26 September	19:30	New Plymouth
Wales		**Namibia**

30 September	20:30	North Harbour, Auckland
South Africa		**Samoa**

2 October	18:00	Hamilton
Wales		**Fiji**

FINAL POOL D TABLE

Pos	Team	P	W	L	D	PF	PA	Pts
D1								
D2								
D3								
D4								
D5								

RUGBY WORLD CUP 2011 FINAL

FINAL 23 October	21:00	Eden Park, Auckland
Winner SF1		Winner SF2

RUGBY WORLD CUP 2011 CHAMPIONS

All kick-offs listed in local New Zealand time.

IRB World Rankings

The IRB World Rankings, introduced in 2003, is a system used to rank the world's international teams based on their results, with all teams given a rating between 0 and 100. The rankings are based on a points-exchange system in which sides take or gain points off each other depending on the result of a match. The points gained or lost in a match depend on the relative strengths of each team and the margin of defeat or victory with an allowance made for teams who have home advantage. Due to the singular importance of the event, points-exchanges are doubled for Rugby World Cup matches.

Pos	Member Union	Rating Point	Pos	Member Union	Rating Point	Pos	Member Union	Rating Point
1	**New Zealand**	**93.19**	33	Kenya	52.85	65	Guyana	41.52
2	Australia	87.45	34	Moldova	52.84	66	China	41.39
3	South Africa	86.44	35	Tunisia	52.24	67	Switzerland	41.36
4	England	82.48	36	Hong Kong	51.57	68	Denmark	41.17
5	Ireland	81.79	37	Poland	51.33	69	Niue Islands	41.11
6	France	81.66	38	Paraguay	50.23	70	Cayman	40.97
7	Scotland	81.20	39	Lithuania	49.83	71	Israel	40.44
8	Argentina	78.97	40	Sweden	49.71	72	Zambia	39.97
9	Wales	77.04	41	Netherlands	48.63	73	Hungary	39.68
10	Fiji	74.05	42	Sri Lanka	48.62	74	India	39.61
11	Samoa	74.02	43	Croatia	48.15	75	St Vincent & the Grenadines	39.30
12	Italy	73.31	44	Uganda	48.13	76	Barbados	39.21
13	Japan	71.45	45	Ivory Coast	47.52	77	Solomon Islands	39.06
14	Canada	69.19	46	Trinidad & Tobago	47.19	78	Cameroon	38.21
15	Georgia	68.21	47	Madagascar	46.45	79	Botswana	38.17
16	United States	67.69	48	Papua New Guinea	46.19	80	St Lucia	37.57
17	Tonga	67.35	49	Zimbabwe	46.15	81	Bulgaria	37.12
18	Russia	65.56	50	Singapore	45.03	82	Austria	36.87
19	Romania	65.54	51	Bermuda	44.74	83	Guam	36.80
20	Uruguay	60.94	52	Cook Islands	44.61	84	Swaziland	36.68
21	Portugal	60.94	53	Malta	44.44	85	Jamaica	36.61
22	Namibia	60.66	54	Latvia	43.85	86	Norway	36.36
23	Spain	58.64	55	Senegal	43.83	87	Bahamas	36.33
24	Chile	56.68	56	Malaysia	43.05	88	Tahiti	36.25
25	Belgium	56.44	57	Andorra	42.91	89	Bosnia & Herzegovina	36.18
26	Morocco	56.11	58	Venezuela	42.88	90	Nigeria	35.29
27	Kazakhstan	55.20	59	Thailand	42.70	91	Monaco	35.17
28	Brazil	54.56	60	Chinese Taipei	42.58	92	Vanuatu	34.77
29	Ukraine	54.35	61	Slovenia	42.12	93	Luxembourg	32.49
30	Germany	54.26	62	Peru	41.98	94	Finland	27.70
31	Czech Republic	53.30	63	Colombia	41.73			
32	Korea	53.03	64	Serbia	41.67			

France's Lionel Nallet and Ireland's Leo Cullen fight for the high ball in 2010. France and Ireland are closely matched in the IRB World Rankings.

The Teams

Twenty teams earned the right to play at Rugby World Cup 2011, 12 through their performances at the 2007 Tournament (the top three teams from each of the four pool groups) and eight via qualifying. The teams will be placed into four groups of five, with each playing the other on a round-robin basis and the top two teams progressing to the quarter-finals. There is plenty to look out for in the Tournament's initial stages: can hosts New Zealand topple their past-Tournament nemesis France in Pool A? Who out of Argentina, England or Scotland will fall at the first hurdle in Pool B? How will Tournament newcomers Russia fare in Pool C? And can Fiji and Wales relive their epic 2007 encounter in Pool D?

England and South Africa run out onto the pitch at the start of Rugby World Cup 2007 Final at Stade de France, Paris.

New Zealand

All Blacks
www.allblacks.com

New Zealand are to Rugby what Brazil are to football: perennially placed towards the top of the IRB World Rankings, a team rated among the favourites for any Tournament they enter and a side that encapsulates the essence of the Game and how it should be played at its very best.

PLAYING STRIP Black shirts, black shorts, black socks with white trim

FORM SINCE RUGBY WORLD CUP 2007

Played:	43
Won:	36
Lost:	7
Drawn:	0
Winning percentage:	83.72
Points for:	1,317
Points against:	676
Points scored per match:	30.62
Points conceded per match:	15.72
Biggest victory:	101–14 v Samoa at New Plymouth on 3 September 2008
Heaviest defeat:	34–19 v Australia at Sydney on 26 July 2008

RUGBY WORLD CUP PERFORMANCES

1987	WORLD CHAMPIONS
1991	Semi-finals
1995	Runners-up
1999	Semi-finals
2003	Semi-finals
2007	Quarter-finals

The greatest irony of the All Blacks' well-documented Rugby World Cup misadventures over the years is that their one moment of triumph, at the inaugural competition in 1987 (for which they were co-hosts with Australia), came at a time when New Zealand Rugby was arguably at its most fractured. In mid-1986, barely 12 months before the start of the Tournament, the All Blacks were left reeling when 28 of the 30-man squad selected for the cancelled 1985 tour to South Africa opted to travel to Africa to play the Springboks on an unofficial, unsanctioned tour of the New Zealand Cavaliers. The fallout may not have been felt on the pitch but the All Blacks' popularity suffered: the New Zealand Rugby public, normally among the most passionate and loyal in the world, lost its patience with the national side. Let alone win the competition, the All Blacks' first task at the 1987 Rugby World Cup was to win those fans back.

The team responded to the challenge in spectacular fashion. They opened up with a comfortable, 12-try demolition of Italy (70–6) at a half-empty Eden Park in Auckland, crushed Fiji 74–13 at a three-quarters-full Lancaster Park in Christchurch and rounded out their pool matches with a 46–15 victory over Argentina at a near-capacity Athletic Park in Wellington. By the time they faced Scotland in the quarter-finals at Christchurch, the Baby Blacks were the hottest ticket in town and they did not disappoint the sell-out crowd when, thanks in no small part to the boot of Grant Fox (with six penalties), they eased to a 30–3 victory. A trip to Brisbane, Australia, for the semi-finals failed to knock them off their stride, as they scored eight tries – two each for John Kirwan and Wayne Shelford – to brush Wales aside en route to a 49–6 victory. Their reward was a final showdown against France – unexpected conquerors of Australia in the semi-finals – at Eden Park and, to the delight of the now-adoring capacity crowd, the match proved a no contest. Tries from Michael Jones, Kirk and Kirwan were enough to see off a lacklustre France. New Zealand ran out 29–9 winners to become Rugby's first world champions. But that is where New Zealand's Rugby World Cup glory ends, making them, to date, one of Rugby's underachievers.

In 1991, a familiar if ageing New Zealand squad was exposed by Australia in the semi-finals and slumped to a 16–6 defeat in Dublin. Four years later, in South Africa, a new generation of All Blacks, inspired by the monstrous presence of Jonah Lomu on the wing, swept all before them on what seemed like an inexorable march to the world crown, only to come unstuck in the Final

COACH

GRAHAM HENRY

Appointed in the aftermath of New Zealand's disappointing semi-final exit to Australia at the 2003 Rugby World Cup, Graham Henry's task as All Blacks coach was simple: to recapture the Game's greatest prize. The former Wales and British & Irish Lions coach duly restored confidence to the All Blacks, leading them to five Tri-Nations crowns in six years and to the top of the world rankings, but his first shot at the Rugby World Cup ended badly: a quarter-final defeat to France and New Zealand's worst-ever Tournament showing. It has to be second time lucky for Henry – who has the unique accolade of being named IRB Coach of the Year a record four times.

STAR PLAYER

JOSEVATA 'JOE' ROKOCOKO

Position:	Wing
Born:	6 June 1983, Nadi, Fiji
Club:	Auckland (NZ)
Height:	1.88m (6ft 2in)
Weight:	104kg (229lb)
Caps:	68
Points:	230 (46t)

Joe Rokocoko was a star at age-group level and made his New Zealand debut a week after turning 20, becoming the youngest All Black since Jonah Lomu. His international career got off to an electrifying start: he scored ten tries in his first ten tests (a strike rate second only to Marc Ellis); was the first All Black to score two or more tries in four consecutive tests; and equalled the world record for the most tries in a calendar year (17). Still only 27, injuries have dulled his pace, but Rokocoko's try-scoring rate is still remarkable (46 in 68 tests). If New Zealand are to lift the Webb Ellis Cup the man they call the 'Rocket Man' must play a major role.

was to follow four years later. Coming into the Tournament off the back of three Tri-Nations successes, comfortably ranked the no.1 side in the world and seen as overwhelming favourites to end what was becoming an embarrassing Rugby World Cup drought, yet again they were undone by unpredictable French flair. As had been the case in 1999, France produced a performance to remember at the Millennium Stadium in Cardiff, winning the quarter-final match 20–18 and condemning the All Blacks to their earliest-ever Tournament exit and a truckload of soul-searching.

The bare facts going into Rugby World Cup 2011 tell a familiar story: New Zealand are the reigning Tri-Nations champions, have only lost seven matches in the last four years, hold a significant lead at the top of the IRB world rankings and, with the likes of Richie McCaw and Dan Carter playing at the peak of their powers, possess the strongest squad on the planet. This time, however, there is optimism for All Blacks fans: for the first time since 1987, New Zealand will have home advantage, and everyone remembers what happened last time. Make no mistake: 2011 will present the All Blacks with their best chance yet to erase the ugliest blight in their Rugby history – their 24-years-and-counting Rugby World Cup drought.

against a South Africa side driven on by an altogether more powerful destiny. As South Africans danced in the streets following their side's 15–12 victory, the All Blacks returned home shell-shocked.

In 1999, with Lomu to the fore once again, the All Blacks romped through their pool matches unbeaten, beat Scotland 30–18 in the quarter-finals and

were firm favourites to beat France in the last four. The French, however, had other ideas, producing an out-of-this-world second-half comeback to win 43–31; the All Blacks had come out on the losing side in what many consider to be the greatest game in history. They suffered semi-final heartache once again in 2003, as Australia outplayed them in Sydney to win 22–10, but worse

PLAYERS TO WATCH

1. **DAN CARTER**
   Age: 29; Position: fly-half; Club: Crusaders (NZ); Caps: 79; Points: 1,188 (29t, 208c, 207p, 2dg)
2. **RICHIE McCAW**
   Age: 30; Position: flanker/captain; Club: Crusaders (NZ); Caps: 94; Points: 95 (19t)
3. **MILS MULIAINA**
   Age: 30; Position: full-back; Club: Chiefs (NZ); Caps: 94; Points: 160 (32t)
4. **MA'A NONU**
   Age: 28; Position: centre; Club: Chiefs (NZ); Caps: 56; Points: 85 (17t)
5. **KIERAN READ**
   Age: 25; Position: No. 8; Club: Crusaders (NZ); Caps: 30; Points: 30 (6t)

The New Zealand All-Blacks perform their famous pre-match *haka*, the Maori dance.

France

Rugby World Cup has been a story of near misses for the French. Despite having produced some of the most scintillating performances in the Tournament's history, they have lost two finals, a statistic they will be trying to put right.

France's Rugby World Cup story did not get off to the most auspicious of starts. Travelling to the southern hemisphere for the inaugural Tournament in 1987 with high hopes, having completed a successful Grand Slam-winning Five Nations campaign, the French crawled to a 20–20 draw against Scotland in their opening match. They recovered with comfortable wins against Romania (55–12) and Zimbabwe (70–12) to top the group on points difference, but they

COACH

MARC LIÈVREMONT

A surprise choice when he was named as coach Bernard Laporte's replacement following the Rugby World Cup 2007, on his appointment former France international Marc Lièvremont vowed to combine pragmatism with open Rugby and an emphasis on developing youth. The formula had mixed results in his first two years, which were marked by experimentation and giving youth its head, but by 2010 he appeared to have settled on his starting line-up, and led France to their first Six Nations Grand Slam success in six years.

desperately needed to up their level of performance. A 31–16 quarter-final win over Fiji was an improvement, and then came Australia, the red-hot pre-Tournament favourites. In what is considered the finest game in Rugby World Cup history, they stunned Australia with a last-gasp Serge Blanco try to steal a famous 30–24 victory. But the victory had taken its toll: from the moment All Black flanker Michael Jones crossed the line for the home side's opening try in the final, there was only going to be one winner. New Zealand eased to a 29–9 victory and France were left to lick their wounds and ponder what might have been.

Having narrowly missed out on the 1991 Five Nations title (England beat them 21–19 in the final Grand Slam showdown), France entered the second Rugby World Cup with high hopes. They topped their group, but the manner of their wins – particularly their 19–13 struggle to beat Canada – left many questions. A quarter-final tie against England was a tougher challenge and, despite home advantage, the French could find no answers as England bullied to a 19–10 win.

Opening victories over the Ivory Coast and Tonga in 1995 set up a clash for top spot against Scotland, and although France scraped to a 22–19 victory, their victory hardly suggested that they were playing at the top of their game. A 36–12 win over Ireland in the quarter-

finals was a return to form, but they were stymied by the weather against hosts South Africa in the semi-final. Torrential rain left the Kings Park pitch saturated – hardly the ideal conditions for France's attacking brand of Rugby – and Les Bleus were edged out 19–15.

France went to the 1999 Tournament with low expectations, having finished last in the Five Nations. But three straight victories in the group stages – albeit against weak opposition – was followed by a comfortable 47–26 victory over Argentina, setting up a semi-final against New Zealand. And that is where everyone expected France's journey to end; instead they produced one of the greatest comebacks in Rugby history

Les Bleus
www.ffr.fr

PLAYING STRIP Blue shirts with white piping, blue shorts, red socks

FORM SINCE RUGBY WORLD CUP 2007
Played:	31
Won:	18
Lost:	13
Drawn:	0
Winning percentage:	58.06
Points for:	665
Points against:	656
Biggest victory:	50–8, v Italy, at Rome on 21 March 2009
Heaviest defeat:	59–16, v Australia, at Stade de France on 27 November 2010
Points scored per match:	21.45
Points conceded per match:	21.16

RUGBY WORLD CUP PERFORMANCES
1987	Runners-up
1991	Quarter-finals
1995	Semi-finals
1999	Runners-up
2003	Semi-finals
2007	Semi-finals

STAR PLAYER

THIERRY DUSAUTOIR

Position: ....Flanker/captain
Born: .18 November 1981, Abidjan, Ivory Coast
Club: ....Toulouse (Fra)
Height: 1.88m (6ft 2in)
Weight: 100.7kg (222lb)
Caps: 37
Points: 25 (5t)

Born in the Ivory Coast, Thierry Dusautoir
moved to France aged ten and took up Rugby
at 16. He played for Bordeaux-Bègles and
Colomiers before joining Biarritz in 2006,
where he reached that year's Heineken Cup
final. He debuted for France the same year
and starred in the Rugby World Cup 2007,
culminating in a sensational, try-scoring
performance against New Zealand in
the quarter-finals – a match in which he
registered an astonishing 36 tackles (two
more than the entire All Blacks side). An ever-
present for Les Bleus since then, he became
captain in November 2009 and led his
country to a Six Nations Grand Slam in 2010.

to stun the All Blacks 43–31 and reach
their second World Cup final. As was
the case in 1987, however, their last-
four exploits had taken their toll, and
Australia cruised to a straightforward
35–12 win.

Expectations were low once more in
2003, but France still managed to cruise
unbeaten through the group stages to
face Ireland in the quarter-finals. The
Irish proved no match and, following a
comprehensive 43–21 victory, France
cantered to a semi-final against England.
But that's where French hopes ended:
on a rainy night in Sydney, France found
themselves on the wrong end of a Jonny

Wilkinson kicking masterclass and
crashed to a 24–7 defeat.

It was a more pragmatic France
that took to the field as hosts in 2007,
but they got off to the worst of starts,
crashing to a 17–12 defeat against
Argentina. They recovered to beat
Namibia, Ireland and Georgia in their
remaining group matches, but the earlier
defeat came at a heavy price: they
would face New Zealand in the quarter-
finals and, worse still, surrendered home
advantage – as the group's runners-up,
they would have to play the match in
Cardiff. However, inspired yet again by
the underdog tag, they produced another
fine performance, coming from 13–3
down at half-time to stun the All Blacks,
the overwhelming pre-Tournament
favourites, 20–18 to book a semi-final
against England. But once again they
buckled: struggling in the face of a
determined English pack and a resolute
Wilkinson boot, they lost 14–9 and the
World Cup dream was over again.

Post 2007, coach Marc Lièvremont
has rung the changes to try to find a
winning formula. In June 2009 they won
in New Zealand for the first time since
2004; in 2010 they achieved their first
Six Nations Grand Slam in six years; and
will travel to the 2011 Rugby World Cup
as the top-ranked northern-hemisphere
side. It is a situation they have been in
before, however, and questions remain
as to whether France can string together
the performances required to capture
Rugby's biggest prize.

France celebrate their 2010 win over Argentina, having lost to the Pumas at Rugby World Cup 2007.

Tonga

POOL A

Although Tonga possess both the natural talent and physical prowess to challenge the Game's top-playing nations, the Sea Eagles have had a bumpy ride at the Rugby World Cup. Four victories in 17 matches in five visits to the Tournament is less than this capable side would want.

The Sea Eagles
www.tongarugbyunion.com

PLAYING STRIP Red shirt with white trim, white shorts, red socks

FORM SINCE RUGBY WORLD CUP 2007

Played:	11
Won:	3
Lost:	8
Drawn:	0
Winning percentage:	27.27
Points for:	249
Points against:	295
Points scored per match:	22.63
Points conceded per match:	26.81
Biggest victory:	27–16 v Fiji
	at Nuku'alofa on 5 July 2008
Heaviest defeat:	35–13 v Japan
	at Sendai on 15 June 2008

RUGBY WORLD CUP PERFORMANCES

1987	Group stages
1991	Did not qualify
1995	Group stages
1999	Group stages
2003	Group stages
2007	Group stages

Tonga hovered beneath world Rugby's radar for decades, playing occasional games against Samoa, Fiji, and the New Zealand Maoris. They first caused a stir in June 1973, beating Australia 16–11 in Brisbane, but then, the odd undistinguished northern hemisphere tour apart, they disappeared back into their South Pacific comfort zone.

So few thought anything out of the ordinary would happen when, in June 1986, Wales stopped off in the Tongan capital Nuku'alofa for the second match of their Pacific Islands tour against the Sea Eagles. For the record, the match ended in a 15–7 victory to the tourists, but the Game will be remembered for much more than that: with minutes to go, play descended into a mass brawl after Wales flanker Mark Brown was flattened by three Tongans. Wales' scrum-half that day, Robert Jones, described the fixture as the dirtiest he had ever played in. A new level of fearlessness was evident in the way Tonga played the Game – and the seed of the islanders' reputation as the hard men of world Rugby was sown.

Eyebrows were raised, then when Tonga were paired in the same group as Wales (alongside Canada and Ireland) at Rugby World Cup 1987,

but the Sea Eagles' performances in the competition did little more than add fuel to the growing debate of the inaugural competition – that there was a staggering gulf between the Game's haves and have-nots. Tonga lost all three of their matches: 37–4 to Canada, 29–16 to Wales and 32–9 to Ireland. The harsh reality was that Tonga had a long way to go if they wanted to compete with the best, and would have to wait eight years before testing their mettle on the Game's biggest stage again.

In Rugby World Cup 1991 qualifiers, Tonga never recovered from their opening-match defeat to Japan (28–16) and, when they fell 12–3 to Samoa, were condemned to missing out on

COACH

ISITOLO MAKA

Still only 35, Isitolo Maka is a former No. 8 who won four caps for the All Blacks (in 1998) and enjoyed a lengthy domestic career in both New Zealand (principally with the Otago Highlanders) and Europe before a persistent knee injury brought an end to his career in 2009 following an outstanding RWC 2007. He was not out of Rugby for long: in 2010 he replaced Quddus Fielea as Tonga's head coach prior to that year's IRB Pacific Nations Cup, in which the Sea Eagles lost all three matches. Much more will be expected of him at Rugby World Cup 2011.

PLAYERS TO WATCH

1. **FANGATAPU 'APIKOTOA** Age: 27; Position: utility back; Club: Coventry (Eng); Caps: 21; Points: 104 (3t, 31c, 9p)
2. **ALIPATE FATAFEHI** Age: 26; Position: wing/centre; Club: North Harbour (NZ); Caps: 6; Points: 15 (3t)
3. **ALEKI LUTUI** Age: 32; Position: hooker; Club: Worcester Warriors (Eng); Caps: 28; Points: 25 (5t)
4. **FINAU MAKA** Age: 33; Position: back row; Club: Aix-en-Provence (Fra); Caps: 4; Points: 5 (1t)
5. **KURT MORATH** Age: 26; Position: fly-half; Club: Southern Districts (NZ); Caps: 4; Points: 50 (2t, 10c, 10p)

The Tongans are looking to convert their physical style of play into wins in 2011.

STAR PLAYER

VUNGA LILO

Position:	Wing
Born:	28 February 1983, Ha'apai, Tonga
Club:	Bordeaux-Bègles (Fra)
Height:	1.93m (6ft 4in)
Weight:	110.2kg (243lb)
Caps:	17
Points:	52 (8t, 4p)

Equally capable at either wing- or full-back, Vunga Lilo made his try-scoring debut for Tonga in the Rugby World Cup 2007 qualifier win over Korea (85–3), repeated the feat in his second game against Japan and scored twice in his third against the Junior All Blacks. He was the star of the show at that years Rugby World Cup, catching the eye with incisive running and capable goal-kicking that helped the Sea Eagles to two victories in the contest for the first time. A journeyman in domestic Rugby, he enjoyed spells in English Rugby with the Cornish Pirates and Bristol and now plies his trade with Bordeaux-Bègles in France.

unravelled to expose Ivory Coast winger Max Brito, paralysed on the ground. Victory may have been sweet for Tonga, but no one was in any mood to celebrate. Instead, the Sea Eagles went home with one searching question: how could they close the gap on the elite Rugby-playing nations?

The Sea Eagles' initial response was to increase their aggression levels, and it was a ferocious Tonga that turned up to Rugby World Cup 1999. They lost their opening match to New Zealand (45–9), showed promise when their physicality proved too much for Italy, grinding out a memorable 28–25 win, then faced England at Twickenham. Pumped up by the prospect that victory over the hosts would secure progress beyond the group stages for the first time, Tonga crossed the line between controlled, intimidating aggression and downright ill-discipline. Prop Ngalu Taufo'ou received his marching orders after knocking England flanker Richard Hill out cold, and the home side cantered to a landslide 101–10 victory. Tonga departed the Tournament under a cloud.

They did little to lift the gloom in 2003. After qualifying with a 194–0 aggregate victory over Korea, they lost all four of their matches. They fared much better in 2007, winning two matches in the Tournament for the first time – against the United States (25–15) and Samoa (19–15) – but, thanks to defeats to South Africa and England, still failed to progress beyond the group stages.

Nobody questions Tonga's huge appetite and passion for the Game, but the problem that has faced the islanders for over a quarter of a century remains: how can they take their game to the next level? Because so many of their players ply their trade at overseas clubs, the Sea Eagles play few international matches – just 11 since the last Rugby World Cup, which is not enough to forge the teamwork and togetherness required to play the Game at the highest level. Tonga will provide bruising opposition for the other teams in Pool A at Rugby World Cup 2011, but it's hard to see them fulfilling their dream of reaching the knockout stages of the competition.

the Tournament for the only time in their history. Qualifying for the 1995 Tournament was an altogether simpler affair: a home-and-away, winner-takes-all showdown against South Pacific neighbours Fiji. Thanks to a convincing, if not surprising, 24–11 away victory in Suva, the Sea Eagles slender 15–10 defeat back in Nuku'alofa mattered little: Tonga were overall 34–26 winners.

Their reward was a place alongside France, Scotland and the Ivory Coast. They slipped to a creditable 38–10 defeat to France and a disappointing 41–5 loss to Scotland before their first-ever win in the Tournament – a 29–11 win over the Ivory Coast. The match, however, was tinged with tragedy: a mere two minutes had been played when a tangled ruck of players

Canada

In Rugby World Cup 1991, when a classy Canada side pushed New Zealand hard, it seemed that the Canucks would take their place among the Game's elite playing nations. But subsequent appearances at the Tournament have been less successful and they are looking to regain their 1991 form.

As an established member of the world Rugby fold – they played their first international match (against Japan) as long ago as 1932 – it came as little surprise when Canada received one of the IRB's 16 invitations to play in the inaugural Rugby World Cup 1987. They made a decent fist of it, too, and lived up to pre-Tournament expectations. They proved too strong for Tonga in their opening match – scoring seven tries in

a 37–4 victory – before losing to Ireland (46–19) and Wales (40–9).

Canada won three of their four matches in the Americas qualifying Tournament (home-and-away fixtures against Argentina and the United States) to earn their place at Rugby World Cup 1991 (although with all three guaranteed a place in the Tournament, the qualifiers served only to rank the sides) and, bolstered by the emergence of class players such as Gareth Rees, 'Stormin' Norman Hadley and Al Charron, arrived in good shape with high hopes. They beat Fiji in their opening match (13–3), edged to victory over Romania (19–11) and, although they lost to France in their final pool match (19–13), did enough to qualify for the quarter-finals. They put up a stiff fight against defending champions New Zealand, only to lose 29–13. It may ultimately have ended in disappointment, but Canada could only have been proud of their efforts: they had reached the competition's last eight for the first time and had given themselves the perfect platform from which to push on.

And that's exactly what they did: in 1993, they recorded victories over an England XV (15–12 at Burnaby Lake) and Wales (26–24 at Cardiff); the following year they celebrated a home victory over France (18–6); and, although they found themselves in the toughest of groups alongside hosts South Africa, Australia and Romania, travelled to Rugby World Cup 1995 with the knowledge that they had the Game, and the players, to provide a stiff examination of the world's best teams. They started well,

beating Romania (34–3) before losing to Australia (27–11). It left Canada needing to win their final pool match, against South Africa, to reach the quarter-finals. They lost the bruising encounter in Port Elizabeth (20–0) and the match was best remembered for the mass brawl that resulted in three players, two of them Canadian (Gareth Rees and Rod Snow), being shown red cards, rather than for the quality of the Rugby.

They qualified for the 1999 Rugby World Cup thanks to two wins out of three – against Uruguay (38–15) and the United States (31–14) – in the Americas qualifying Tournament, but the manner of their one defeat, 54–28 to Argentina,

The Canucks/Maple Leafs
www.rugbycanada.ca

PLAYING STRIP Red shirts with black and white trim, black shorts, black socks

FORM SINCE RUGBY WORLD CUP 2007

Played:	18
Won:	9
Lost:	9
Drawn:	0
Winning percentage:	50.00
Points for:	403
Points against:	411
Points scored per match:	22.39
Points conceded per match:	22.83
Biggest victory:	48–6 v Uruguay at Glendale on 5 June 2010
Heaviest defeat:	55–0 v Ireland at Limerick on 8 November 2008

RUGBY WORLD CUP PERFORMANCES

1987	Group stages
1991	Quarter-finals
1995	Group stages
1999	Group stages
2003	Group stages
2007	Group stages

STAR PLAYER

D.T.H. VAN DER MERWE

Position:	Wing/centre
Born:	28 April 1986, Worcester, South Africa
Club:	Glasgow Warriors (Sco)
Height:	1.83m (6ft)
Weight:	91.6kg (202lb)
Caps:	15
Points:	50 (10t)

Born in Worcester, South Africa, Daniel Tailliferre Hauman (known as 'D.T.H.') van der Merwe started playing Rugby at the age of five and went on to play for the Boland U16 team before his family emigrated to Regina, Canada in 2003. Playing for Saskatchewan U18s and U21s, he debuted for Canada in their Rugby World Cup qualifying match against Barbados in 2006 (he scored two tries). Ven der Merwe started in all four of Canada's games at Rugby World Cup 2007 and, still only 24 years old, has remained one of the first names on the Canucks' teamsheet. He has played his club Rugby with the Glasgow Warriors in Scotland since 2009.

should have caused concern. The Pumas can certainly be a formidable force on home soil, but this represented Canada's third straight defeat against Argentina,

Canada will be looking to carry their qualifying form into the Tournament itself.

a side who, like Canada, had their own aspirations of settling among the world's elite playing nations. Perhaps some of Canada's old guard was losing its edge. That suspicion was confirmed when, in the Tournament itself, the Canucks crashed to two defeats in their first two games – against France (33–20) and Fiji (38–22) – and their one victory (72–11 against Namibia) gave few crumbs of comfort. Canada's Rugby fortunes had taken a turn for the worse.

There was little cause for cheer in 2003 either. Yet again, Canada qualified for the Tournament with ease, winning five of their six matches (losing only away to Uruguay, 25–23), but, once they had arrived in Australia, they crashed to defeat in their first three games – against Wales (41–10), New Zealand (68–6) and Italy (19–14). With any hopes of progressing beyond the group already quashed, a final-match victory over Tonga (24–7) was scant consolation.

They achieved a 100 per cent record in qualification for Rugby World Cup 2007, but it made little difference to

their performance in the Tournament. They opened up with two straight defeats – against Wales (42–17) and Fiji (29–16) – recorded a disappointing 12–12 draw against Japan and crashed out of the Tournament following a 37–6 loss to Australia. It was the first time in their history that they had failed to win a single match in the Tournament.

It was time for a change. Out went coach Ric Suggitt, who had been in charge since February 2004, and, in March 2008, in came Kieran Crowley, the Kiwi who had taken the New Zealand U19s to IRB Under 19 World Championship glory in 2007. The appointment was undoubtedly a coup and the former Taranaki coach was quick to state his intentions. 'My impression [of the team] at the moment is that they are a very physical team and have very good set-piece plays. The area that needs improvement is the vision to change things when they are not as structured as they should be.' But results have not gone Canada's way since then, losing to Wales, Ireland, Scotland and Georgia. Given the quality of their Pool A opponents, it's hard to see Canada causing any major shocks at Rugby World Cup 2011. Victories over Tonga and Japan would be a decent result for a side that is rebuilding on the international stage.

PLAYERS TO WATCH

1. **AARON CARPENTER** – Age: 27; Position: back row; Club: Plymouth Albion (Eng); Caps: 32; Points: 25 (5t)
2. **ADAM KLEEBERGER** – Age: 26; Position: flanker; Club: Auckland (NZ); Caps: 27; Points: 25 (5t)
3. **ANDER MONRO** – Age: 29; Position: fly-half; Club: Ontario Blues (Can); Caps: 22; Points: 32 (1t, 6c, 4p, 1dg)
4. **JAMES PRITCHARD** – Age: 31; Position: full-back/wing; Club: Northampton Saints (Eng); Caps: 33; Points: 332 (12t, 61c, 50p)
5. **PAT RIORDAN** – Age: 31; Position: hooker/captain; Club: Burnaby Lake (Can); Caps: 32; Points: 20 (4t)

Japan

Japan are the kings of Asian Rugby and are the only team from the continent to have appeared at a Rugby World Cup, but whereas they have lost only once to another Asian team in the last decade, the Cherry Blossoms have found victories on the Game's greatest stage harder to come by.

The Cherry Blossoms
www.rugbyjapan.com

PLAYING STRIP Dark red shirts with white hoops, black shorts, black socks

FORM SINCE RUGBY WORLD CUP 2007

Played:	27
Won:	21
Lost:	6
Drawn:	0
Winning percentage:	77.77
Points for:	1,344
Points against:	429
Points scored per match:	49.78
Points conceded per match:	15.89
Biggest victory:	114–6 v Arabian Gulf at Osaka on 3 May 2008
Heaviest defeat:	34–15 v Samoa at Sigatoka on 18 June 2009

RUGBY WORLD CUP PERFORMANCES

1987	Group stages
1991	Group stages
1995	Group stages
1999	Group stages
2003	Group stages
2007	Group stages

One of the more surprising aspects of Japanese Rugby is the sheer popularity of the Game: only England, South Africa, France and Australia (in that order) have more registered senior players than Japan's 129,626. That is because Japan and Rugby share a long history. Brought to the islands in 1874 by British sailors, Rugby soon found popularity: by 1899 it was played by students in Kaio University; by 1926 the Japan Rugby Football Union had been formed; and, six years later, Japan played their first-ever international match, against Canada (they won 9–8).

With Rugby slow to spread throughout Asia, the Cherry Blossoms' early years of international Rugby saw them restricted to playing against often-weakened touring teams – with moderate success (they won only 13 of their first 50 matches) – and it wasn't until the inaugural Rugby World Cup 1987 that they had a genuine chance to test their mettle against full-strength international opponents. They made a decent fist of it, losing narrowly to the United States (21–18), heavily to England (60–7) and creditably to Australia (42–23).

They lost their opening two games at Rugby World Cup 1991, too, against Scotland (47–9) and Ireland (32–16), but then came a significant day in Japan's Rugby history. They ran in nine tries in a 52–8 victory over Zimbabwe: nobody knew it, but it was the first and last time Japan tasted victory.

If their performances at the 1991 Tournament had been encouraging, however, their displays in South Africa four years later were chastening. Defeats to Scotland (57–10) and Ireland (50–28) may not have raised any eyebrows, but even the most pessimistic could not have foreseen the disaster that awaited in the final pool match

against New Zealand. The All Blacks, so confident that they rested the majority of their star players, fielded a second-string XV that still proved too much for Japan, running in a staggering 21 tries in a 145–17 win that left the Cherry Blossoms' reputation in ruins. 4 June 1995 remains the darkest day in Japan's Rugby history. The match exposed their greatest flaw: swift of hand and fleet of foot in attack and tenacious in defence are no match for the physicality of the world's best.

Licking their wounds, Japan retreated to the comfort zone of Asian Rugby and suffered three straight defeats to Hong Kong for the first and only time in their history. Although they recorded a 100

COACH

JOHN KIRWAN

A Rugby World Cup winner as a player with New Zealand in 1987, John Kirwan cut his coaching teeth with Italy, who he took to the Rugby World Cup 2003. He took over as Japan coach prior to the 2007 Tournament and has embarked on a campaign of rebuilding and looking to the future as Japan prepares to host Rugby World Cup 2019. The reigning Asian 5 Nations champions enjoyed a stellar IRB Pacific Nations Cup campaign in 2010 and will be looking to take another step forward in New Zealand.

Japan are the kings of Asian Rugby and have participated in every Rugby World Cup.

After qualifying for the 2007 Tournament, Japan pulled off a coup by securing John Kirwan as coach. The former All Black had done a good job with Italy, adding steel to the Azzurri's game. Prior to Rugby World Cup 2007, Kirwan stated Japan's Tournament objective: to beat Canada and Fiji. It was a failed mission: Japan went winless for the fifth consecutive time, losing to Australia (91–3), Fiji (35–31) and Wales (72–18) before securing a 12–12 draw with Canada to end their 13-game losing streak. There was still work to do.

As he had done with Italy, Kirwan's first move was to broaden the net to include players who qualified through residency (such as foreign professionals who had made a career on Japan's thriving domestic circuit). And with a home Rugby World Cup in 2019 to look forward to, the Cherry Blossoms seem to have made significant strides. In 2010, they recorded two victories in the Pacific Nations Cup for the first time, with wins over eventual champions Samoa (31–23) and Tonga (26–23), and rounded out the year with a big win over Rugby World Cup 2011 qualifiers Russia (75–3). The Cherry Blossoms will be focusing on their Pool A matches against Canada and Tonga as the ones in which they can end their 20-year winless streak, and nobody should bet against them winning at least one of those games.

STAR PLAYER

TAKASHI KIKUTANI

Position:	Back row/captain
Born:	24 February 1980, Nara, Japan
Club:	Toyota Verblitz (Jap)
Height:	1.88m (6ft 2in)
Weight:	99.8kg (220lb)
Caps:	33
Points:	90 (18t)

Recently named in the top 15 players in Japan's domestic league, Takashi Kikutani made a try-scoring debut for Japan against Spain in 2005, and his combative approach soon saw him become a regular. He missed out on Rugby World Cup 2007, but when John Kirwan started to ring the changes after the Tournament, Kikutani's form became impossible to ignore. Appointed national captain in March 2009, he has led the Cherry Blossoms in talismanic fashion, scoring 16 tries in his last 22 internationals (a remarkable try-scoring rate for a forward) and helping Japan to secure a seventh successive appearance at the Rugby World Cup.

PLAYERS TO WATCH

1. **JAMES ARLIDGE** Age: 31; Position: fly-half; Club: Nottingham (Eng); Caps: 22; Points: 188 (5t, 53c, 18p, 1dg)
2. **RYAN NICHOLAS** Age: 31; Position: centre/fly-half; Club: Suntory Sungoliath (Jap); Caps: 23; Points: 154 (5t, 45c, 13p)
3. **HITOSHI ONO** Age: 32; Position: lock; Club: Toshiba Brave Lupus (Jap); Caps: 43; Points: 30 (6t)
4. **HIROTOKI ONOZAWA** Age: 32; Position: wing/full-back; Club: Suntory Sungoliath (Jap); Caps: 57; Points: 200 (40t)
5. **BRYCE ROBINS** Age: 30; Position: centre/fly-half; Club: NEC Green Rockets (Jap); Caps: 22; Points: 62 (12t, 1c)

per cent record in qualifying for Rugby World Cup 1999, they travelled to the Tournament with little hope of ending their losing streak. Yet again they lost all three matches: to Samoa (43–9), Wales (64–15) and Argentina (33–12).

Japan's path to redemption – in the eyes of their fans, at least – started with a world record-equalling 155–3 win over Chinese Taipei in Rugby World Cup 2003

qualifiers, and although they would go on to lose all of their matches for the fourth Tournament in a row – against Scotland (32–11), France (51–29), Fiji (41–13) and, most disappointingly of all, against the United States (39–26) – their fast-flowing, attacking brand of Rugby thrilled fans and left many hailing the Cherry Blossoms as the best of the world's so-called emerging teams.

WESTERN SAMOA SHOCK WALES
6 OCTOBER 1991, CARDIFF ARMS PARK, CARDIFF

For Wales it was the most important fixture in the national team's 110-year history; for Western Samoa, their first-ever Rugby World Cup match represented a unique opportunity to shine on the Game's biggest stage. And how they shone, knocking Wales out of their stride with a ferocious tackling display and taking the lead through a Matthew Vaea penalty. Wales replied with a penalty of their own and the score was locked at 3–3 at the interval. The Samoans made an emphatic start to the second half, establishing a 9–3 lead through a converted To'o Vaega try 35 seconds after the restart and moved 13–3 ahead when Sila Vaifale crossed the line. Wales rallied to make it 13–9, but Samoa's Vaea kicked a penalty to make it 16–9 and the islanders hung on to win 16–13 and record the biggest shock in the Tournament's history.

The Wales and Samoan forwards lock horns during Wales' shock defeat in 1991.

Argentina

Argentina are Rugby World Cup's greatest success story: they used the Tournament to transform themselves from the giants of South American Rugby into a side that is riding high in the IRB World Rankings. They are now major contenders and will make their Four Nations bow in 2012.

The Pumas
www.uar.com.ar

PLAYING STRIP Light blue and white hooped shirts, white shorts, light blue and white socks

FORM SINCE RUGBY WORLD CUP 2007
Played:	21
Won:	9
Lost:	12
Drawn:	0
Winning percentage:	42.86
Points for:	431
Points against:	401
Points scored per match:	20.52
Points conceded per match:	19.10
Biggest victory:	79–8 v Chile
at San Juan on 15 December 2007	
Heaviest defeat:	63–9 v South Africa
at Johannesburg on 9 August 2008	

RUGBY WORLD CUP PERFORMANCES
1987	Group stages
1991	Group stages
1995	Group stages
1999	Quarter-finals
2003	Group stages
2007	Semi-finals

Not that the Pumas' transformation was an instant affair. They travelled to the inaugural Rugby World Cup 1987 with a growing reputation and were a team looking to kick on to the next level of the world game. That reputation lay in tatters following a surprise opening-game 29–8 defeat to Fiji and, although the Pumas rallied to beat Italy (25–16) in their second match, nothing short of victory in their final pool match – against New Zealand – would be enough for them to progress to the semi-finals. The All Blacks cantered to a 46–15 victory and Argentina's interest in the Tournament came to an abrupt end.

It was a new-look Argentina that travelled to the second Rugby World Cup in 1991, but they lost all three matches – against Australia (32–19), Wales (16–7) and, disappointingly, Samoa (35–12).

The world got its first glimpse of what would become the template for Argentina Rugby at Rugby World Cup 1995. Placed in a tough group alongside England, Italy and Samoa, they lost all three matches, albeit slenderly (24–18 to England, 32–26 to Samoa and 31–25 to Italy), but it was the dominance of the Pumas' pack in all three matches that indicated signs of improvement.

Encouraged by their performances in South Africa, Argentina travelled to Rugby World Cup 1999 as a team with a defined gameplan. They lost their opening match against hosts Wales (23–18), but rallied to beat Japan (32–16) and Samoa (33–12) to earn a playoff against Ireland for a place in the quarter-finals. In what counts as the Pumas' greatest achievement in the Tournament to that date, they won 28–24. The journey came to an end with a 47–26 last-eight defeat to France.

COACH

SANTIAGO PHELAN

A former back-row forward who won 44 caps for the Pumas between 1997 and 2003 (and who appeared at both Rugby World Cups 1999 and 2003) before retiring aged 29 through injury, Phelan cut his coaching teeth with Buenos Aires giants CASI and Argentina A before, in March 2008, he was asked to fill the giant void created by Marcelo Loffreda's decision to step down as Pumas' head coach. Still only 35, he will have to steer an ageing Argentina side through a second successive Rugby World Cup.

They almost repeated their 1999 performance four years later. They lost to hosts Australia in the opening game (24–8), but bounced back to record convincing wins over Namibia (67–14) and Romania (50–3) to set up a showdown against Ireland, with the winner progressing to the quarter-finals as the group runners-up. On this occasion Ireland won to avenge the defeat they had suffered four years earlier but nevertheless the Pumas' improvement was obvious.

The Pumas' form going into Rugby World Cup 2007 had been the talk of world Rugby. In November 2004, they had beaten France 24–14 in Marseille;

STAR PLAYER

JUAN MARTÍN FERNÁNDEZ LOBBE

Position: ....No. 8
Born: .... 19 November 1981, Buenos Aires,
....Argentina
Club: ....Toulon (Fra)
Height: 1.93m (6ft 4in)
Weight: 102kg (225lb)
Caps: 39
Points: 20 (4t)

Buenos Aires-born Juan Martín Fernández Lobbe made his international debut in 2004 but it wasn't until he moved to English club side Sale Sharks in 2006 that he rose to international prominence. A versatile back-row forward, he scored a try in each of Argentina's 2006 victories over Wales, helped the Pumas to an historic win over England and played a prominent role in their Rugby World Cup 2007 campaign. He led his country for the first time in November 2008 and again the following year in the Pumas' 24–22 home victory over England. He moved to French club side Toulon in 2009.

the following year, they held the British & Irish Lions to a 25–25 draw in Cardiff and beat Scotland 23–19 at Murrayfield; in June 2006, they recorded back-to-back home victories over Wales and rounded out the year with a headline-grabbing 25–18 victory over England at Twickenham. The Pumas had developed a style of play – and a group of talented players who were capable of executing

it – that was capable of challenging any side in the world.

The convincing nature of Argentina's performances in the 2007 Tournament was a surprise. They got off to a flying start at the Stade de France when they beat hosts France 17–12 in their opening game. The good form continued with comfortable victories over Georgia (33–3) and Namibia (63–3), but then

came the next test: a final pool match against Ireland which would give the Pumas an opportunity to win their pool, eliminate Ireland and prove that their performance against France had not been a fluke. They responded magnificently and secured a famous 30–15 victory. The dream run continued with a 19–13 victory over Scotland in the quarter-finals. In the blink of an eye Argentina had made it to the semi-finals of Rugby World Cup 2007. But their golden journey ended there. The Springboks matched the Pumas' forward dominance where others had failed and coasted to a 37–13 victory.

However they beat France 34–10 in the third-place playoff; leapt to number three in the world rankings and were handed the chance to join an expanded Tri-Nations championship. Argentina had arrived in Rugby's big time. Considerable pressure has been placed on the Pumas since those heady days in the summer of 2007 and their post-Rugby World Cup form has been patchy with a number of notable retirees, with home victories over under-strength England and France sides their only performances of note. Drawn in a tough group, the Pumas match against Scotland could well decide which of those two countries will progress to the quarter-finals, but it would be a major achievement if Argentina progressed any further.

PLAYERS TO WATCH

1. **PATRICIO ALBACETE** Age: 29; Position: lock; Club: Toulouse (Fra); Caps: 40; Points: 5 (1t)
2. **FELIPE CONTEPOMI** Age: 33; Position: centre/fly-half; Club: Toulon (Fra); Caps: 70; Points: 557 (13t, 60c, 121p, 3dg)
3. **JUAN MARTÍN HERNÁNDEZ** Age: 28; Position: fly-half; Club: Racing Métro (Fra); Caps: 32; Points: 83 (6t, 4c, 9p, 6dg)
4. **RODRIGO RONCERO** Age: 33; Position: prop; Club: Stade Français (Fra); Caps: 43; Points: 20 (4t)
5. **MARTÍN SCELZO** Age: 34; Position: prop; Club: Clermont Auvergne; Caps: 53; Points: 45 (9t)

The Pumas are looking to regain the fantastic form they demonstrated at the 2007 Tournament.

England

England have been slow to regain their World Cup-winning form under former captain Martin Johnson's charge but seem to be hitting their stride heading into Rugby World Cup year. Their recent pedigree in the competition suggests the 2003 champions will be a major contender in New Zealand.

England
www.rfu.com

PLAYING STRIP White shirts with grey trim, white shorts, black socks

FORM SINCE RUGBY WORLD CUP 2007

Played:	32
Won:	14
Lost:	17
Drawn:	1
Winning percentage:	45.31
Points for:	633
Points against:	635
Points scored per match:	19.78
Points conceded per match:	19.84
Biggest victory:	39–13 v Pacific Islanders at Twickenham on 8 November 2008
Heaviest defeat:	42–6 v South Africa at Twickenham on 22 November 2008

RUGBY WORLD CUP PERFORMANCES

1987	Quarter-finals
1991	Runners-up
1995	Semi-finals
1999	Quarter-finals
2003	WORLD CHAMPIONS
2007	Runners-up

England travelled to the Tournament in 1987 with low expectations, having just finished bottom of the Five Nations Championship. They lost their opening match to Australia (19–6) and, although they showed glimpses of promise in comfortable victories over Japan (60–7) and the United States (34–6), produced a poor display against Wales in the quarter-finals and were dumped out of the competition following a 16–3 defeat.

COACH

MARTIN JOHNSON

Martin Johnson's appointment as England's head coach in April 2008 was not met with universal acclaim: no one questioned the former captain's leadership skills (he is the only player in history to have captained the British & Irish Lions on two tours and led England to Rugby World Cup glory in 2003), rather the wisdom of handing the reins of the national side to a man with zero coaching experience. Slowly, however, Johnson has proved his critics wrong, blending youth with experience to create a side cast in his own image that seems to be hitting form.

In contrast, it was a vibrant England that entered the 1991 Tournament. Revitalized under the captaincy of Will Carling, fresh off the back of a Grand Slam-winning Five Nations campaign and aided by home advantage, hopes were high. Even an 18–12 defeat to New Zealand in their opening game did little to dampen the sense of expectation and England regrouped well, stuck to their forward-oriented gameplan and finished as group runners-up thanks to solid victories over Italy (36–6) and the United States (37–9).

Next up was a quarter-final clash against France in Paris – a sure test of any team's credentials. In a memorably bruising encounter that saw England at their harrying best they secured an impressive 19–10 victory. Their reward was a semi-final clash against Scotland at Murrayfield which the visitors edged 9–6 in a nervy victory that earned them a place in the final against Australia at Twickenham.

It could be that David Campese's pre-match observation that they were a one-dimensional team spurred them on or that they found the prospect of winning the Game's greatest prize on home soil in style too alluring, but, for whatever reason, England abandoned the pack-led gameplan that had served them so well throughout the Tournament and opted for a more expansive game in the final. It backfired: Australia scored the only try of the Game and held out wave after wave of increasingly desperate England attack to win the

match 12–6. England had missed a huge opportunity.

After winning their group with three straight victories, albeit unconvincing ones – against Argentina (24–18), Italy (27–20) and Samoa (44–22), England gained some measure of revenge when they beat Australia 25–22 in the quarter-finals of Rugby World Cup 1995, but the overriding memory of that Tournament was their crushing 45–29 semi-final defeat to a Jonah Lomu-inspired New Zealand – the giant winger scoring four of the All Blacks' six tries. More disappointment was to follow in 1999: England progressed to the quarter-finals only to be undone by another display of individual brilliance as

STAR PLAYER

LEWIS MOODY

Position: ....Flanker/captain
Born: ....12 June 1978, Ascot, England
Club: ....Bath (Eng)
Height: 1.92m (6ft 3in)
Weight: 102.9kg (227lb)
Caps: 66
Points: 45 (9t)

Lewis Moody is a firebrand of a flanker who has made his name putting his body on the line for his team's cause. He started with Leicester Tigers, making his first-team debut in 1996, but had to wait five years before making his full England debut, against Canada in 2001. He played a part in every game in England's Rugby World Cup 2003 winning team. He played for the British & Irish Lions in 2005 then struggled with injuries before fighting back to retain his place in the England side for the 2009 autumn internationals. Having won every honour in the Game, his appointment as England captain in 2010 has proved inspired.

the quarter-finals and ground out a solid 24–7 victory over France in the semi-finals (with Wilkinson kicking all of England's points). They produced a nervy performance against Australia in the final, but held their nerve when it mattered to secure a 20–17 victory and the title of world champions – becoming the first team from the northern hemisphere to do so.

A series of retirements, two changes of coach and a catalogue of injuries to their star player meant that few thought England had any chance of retaining their world crown in 2007 and that feeling was reinforced when they capitulated to a 36–0 defeat to South Africa in their second pool match. It was the hiding England needed: stirred into action, they won their final two pool matches, beat Australia (12–10) in the quarter-finals and out-muscled France (14–9) in the semi-finals to reach their second successive Rugby World Cup Final, against South Africa. England fared better this time round and had their chances to win, but South Africa held out for a deserved 15–6 victory.

England seem set to start Rugby World Cup 2011 in both better form and higher spirits than was the case in 2007, but they will have to be at their absolute best if they are to become the first team in the Tournament's history to reach three successive World Cup Finals.

England are now back in their stride and are hopeful of a third successive Final in 2011.

South Africa's Jannie de Beer slotted an unprecedented five drop-goals to help the Springboks to a 44–21 victory.

The manner of the defeat to South Africa prompted coach Clive Woodward to turn a talented squad into the best-prepared unit in world Rugby and, led by the indomitable Martin Johnson and with a supremely talented fly-half in Jonny Wilkinson at their disposal, England

started to turn things round and travelled to Rugby World Cup 2003 as the world's No. 1 ranked team. They duly lived up to the hype.

They eased through their group, recording comfortable victories over Georgia (84–6), South Africa (25–6), Samoa (35–22) and Uruguay (111–13), produced a stirring second-half display to see off Wales (28–17) in

PLAYERS TO WATCH

1. **CHRIS ASHTON** Age: 23; Position: wing; Club: Northampton Saints (Eng); Caps: 7; Points: 15 (3t)
2. **TOM CROFT** Age: 25; Position: flanker; Club: Leicester Tigers (Eng); Caps: 22; Points: 5 (1t)
3. **BEN FODEN** Age: 25; Position: full-back; Club: Northampton Saints (Eng); Caps: 10; Points: 10 (2t)
4. **ANDREW SHERIDAN** Age: 31; Position: prop; Club: Sale Sharks (Eng); Caps: 36; Points: 0
5. **BEN YOUNGS** Age: 21; Position: scrum-half; Club: Leicester Tigers (Eng); Caps: 7; Points: 5 (1t)

Scotland

With a smaller pool of players to choose from than either Tonga or Samoa, Scotland could be considered the greatest overachievers in Rugby World Cup history, having progressed beyond the group stages in each of their six appearances at the Tournament.

Scotland
www.scottishrugby.org

PLAYING STRIP Blue shirts with white trim, blue shorts, blue socks

FORM SINCE RUGBY WORLD CUP 2007

Played:	28
Won:	11
Lost:	16
Drawn:	1
Winning percentage:	41.07
Points for:	447
Points against:	540
Points scored per match:	15.96
Points conceded per match:	19.29
Biggest victory:	41–0 v Canada
at Aberdeen on 22 November 2008	
Heaviest defeat:	49–3 v New Zealand
at Murrayfield on 13 November 2010	

RUGBY WORLD CUP PERFORMANCES

1987	Quarter-finals
1991	Semi-finals
1995	Quarter-finals
1999	Quarter-finals
2003	Quarter-finals
2007	Quarter-finals

Scotland's Rugby World Cup 1987 adventure started well, securing a 20–20 draw in their opening pool match against reigning Five Nations champions France. These two teams dominated their pool (the other teams, Zimbabwe and Romania, were outgunned) which meant that the group winner would be decided by points difference. France topped the pool, finishing with a points difference of +101 to Scotland's +66. It made a crucial difference: second place condemned Scotland to a quarter-final match against the All Blacks in Christchurch – a formidable test. The New Zealanders ran out comfortable 30–3 winners.

The Scotland camp was in similarly high spirits going into Rugby World Cup 1991. Just a year before they had stunned England 13–7 in an epic, encounter to secure a memorable Grand Slam and, with the prospect of being able to play all of their matches up to the final at Murrayfield (a ground where they had not lost since 1988), the Scots knew they had a great chance of progressing deep into the competition. They opened with comfortable wins over Japan (47–9) and Zimbabwe (51–12) and then faced a crunch encounter against Ireland, with top spot in the group up for grabs. Scotland scored two tries to Ireland's none and won the match 24–15. Their reward was a quarter-final clash against Samoa, a bruising encounter they won 28–6 and next in the firing line were England.

In what turned out to be a nervy affair, the Scots found themselves trailing 9–6 with only minutes to go. Miraculously, they were awarded a penalty in front of the posts in England's 22 and were handed the chance to take the match into extra-time. But disaster struck: Gavin Hastings misfired and Scotland were left to contemplate what might have been.

They travelled to South Africa in 1995 in good form, having finished as runners-up to England in that year's Five Nations, and started their campaign with a comfortable 89–0 victory over Tournament newcomers Ivory Coast. They proved too strong for Tonga, too, winning 41–5 to set up a pool-deciding final match against France – a team they had beaten 23–21 in Paris only months earlier. But the French won 22–19 and defeat left Scotland with a daunting consolation: a quarter-final clash against New Zealand. The Scots performed admirably but the All Blacks ran out effortless 48–30 winners. It was a familiar story in 1999: Scotland went into the Tournament as

COACH

ANDY ROBINSON

Capped eight times for England, Andy Robinson cut his teeth as a coach first with Bath Rugby (1997–2000), winning the Heineken Cup in 1998, and then as the assistant coach with England. An obvious replacement for Sir Clive Woodward when the Rugby World Cup-winning coach resigned in 2004, Robinson endured a tough run and was sacked in 2006. He has since worked in Scottish Rugby, first with Edinburgh and the Scotland A side (2007–2009) and, since June 2009, as the head coach of an improving national team.

STAR PLAYER

ROSS FORD

Position: .... Hooker
Born: .... 23 April 1984, Edinburgh, Scotland
Club: ....Edinburgh (Sco)
Height: 1.85m (6ft 1in)
Weight: 109.8kg (242lb)
Caps: 43
Points: 10 (2t)

Ross Ford graduated through the ranks of junior international Rugby and switched from flanker to hooker after signing for Scottish club side Border Reivers in 2004. He made his senior international debut (against Australia) later the same year. Fifteen months would pass before he won his second cap, but after a strong domestic campaign in 2006 he won his first start for Scotland in 2007, won a place in Scotland's squad for Rugby World Cup 2007 and made the Scotland No. 2 jersey his own. His standout performances brought him a British & Irish Lions cap in 2009.

It is a pattern the Scots have been unable to break. In 2003, they beat Japan (32–11), the United States (39–15) and Fiji (22–20) as expected, but lost the match that really mattered, against France (51–9), to finish second in their group. This time they faced hosts Australia in the quarter-finals and lost 33–16. Four years later, they beat Portugal (56–10), Romania (42–0) and Italy (18–16), lost to New Zealand (40–0) and again fell at the quarter-final stage, 19–13 to Argentina.

Scottish Rugby has ebbed and flowed since then. After a lean spell in the Six Nations, Andy Robinson replaced Frank Hadden as coach in June 2009, and in November that year they beat Australia (9–8) at Murrayfield; in 2010 they produced their best Six Nations campaign for years, beating Ireland (23–20), drawing with England (15–15) and had Wales on the ropes before losing 31–24. This was followed by a pair of away victories over Argentina in June 2010 and a 21–17 home victory over South Africa in the autumn confirmed that considerable progress had been made.

Scotland's task at Rugby World Cup 2011 will be a difficult one: they will have to win at least one of their matches against Argentina and England if they want to preserve their record of having reached at least the quarter-finals at every Rugby World Cup. It is a task the revived Scots are more than capable of achieving.

reigning Five Nations champions and, although they had been placed in a tough group alongside South Africa, would play all of their pool matches at Murrayfield. They failed to make home advantage count in the opening match against the Springboks and lost

46–29. It was the seminal moment of Scotland's Tournament: they may have beaten Uruguay (43–12) and Spain (48–0) to finish as group runners-up and then beaten Samoa (35–20) in the quarter-final playoff match, but their opening defeat came with a familiar consequence: a quarter-final tie against New Zealand. The All Blacks won the match, this time 30–18.

PLAYERS TO WATCH

1. **JOHNNIE BEATTIE** Age: 25; Position: No. 8; Club: Glasgow Warriors (Sco); Caps: 14; Points: 15 (3t)
2. **NATHAN HINES** Age: 34; Position: lock/flanker; Club: Leinster (Ire); Caps: 67; Points: 10 (2t)
3. **SEAN LAMONT** Age: 30; Position: wing; Club: Scarlets (Wal); Caps: 50; Points: 35 (7t)
4. **EUAN MURRAY** Age: 30; Position: prop; Club: Northampton Saints (Eng); Caps: 35; Points: 10 (2t)
5. **DAN PARKS** Age: 32; Position: fly-half; Club: Cardiff Blues (Wal); Caps: 56; Points: 207 (4t, 11c, 42p, 13dg)

Scotland's record in previous Rugby World Cups plus good current form is cause for optimism.

Georgia

Georgia's national Rugby team has come a long way since the country gained political independence in 1991 and have won Europe's second-tier Tournament (the European Nations Cup) twice in succession. They are preparing to appear in their third Rugby World Cup.

The Lelos
www.rugby.ge

PLAYING STRIP White shirts with red trim, white shorts, white socks

FORM SINCE RUGBY WORLD CUP 2007

Played:	22
Won:	17
Lost:	4
Drawn:	1
Winning percentage:	79.55
Points for:	552
Points against:	327
Points scored per match:	25.09
Points conceded per match:	14.86
Biggest victory:	77–3 v Germany at Tbilisi on 6 February 2010
Heaviest defeat:	42–10 v Canada at Glendale on 6 June 2009

RUGBY WORLD CUP PERFORMANCES

1987	Did not enter
1991	Did not enter
1995	Did not qualify
1999	Did not qualify
2003	Group stages
2007	Group stages

'The Lelos' played their first official international against the Ukraine, on 21 November 1991 and won 19–15. They first tried to qualify for Rugby World Cup 1995, but defeats to Russia (15–9) and Poland (23–6) saw their campaign halted.

They fared much better in Rugby World Cup 1999 qualifying Tournament, winning three of four games in the initial group stage (Round B) – beating Croatia (19–15), Denmark (19–8) and Russia (12–6) but losing to Italy (31–14) – to progress to Round C. They lost to Ireland (70–0) and to Romania (27–23) to miss out on an automatic qualifying spot. There was still hope, however, as they progressed to the repechage round against Tonga. They lost 37–6 in the Tongan capital Nuku'alofa and won 28–27 in Tbilisi to crash out of the Tournament 64–34 on aggregate.

This narrow miss provided a huge confidence boost and, under new French coach Claude Saurel, they finished second in the European Nations Cup in 2000. The following year, they shocked Romania in Bucharest (31–20) to win the Trophy for the first time; and, in 2001, when Georgia finished a creditable tenth in the Sevens Rugby World Cup, interest in the Game started to explode. If such momentum was to be maintained, however, Georgia would have to qualify for the following year's Rugby World Cup.

Their bid to do so started in disappointing fashion against Ireland at Lansdowne Road: the home side ran in eight tries to Georgia's two to win 63–14. That left the Lelos facing a crunch match against Russia, with the winner guaranteed a place at Rugby World Cup 2003. On 13 October 2002, roared on by a 50,000 crowd in Tbilisi, Georgia held their nerve to beat their archrivals 17–13 to secure a place among the Game's elite for the first time. It remains the proudest day in Georgia's Rugby history.

The Tournament itself, however, turned out to be a chastening experience. The

COACH

RICHIE DIXON

Given that his predecessor, Tim Lane, had just helped Georgia secure qualification for their third successive Rugby World Cup and guided them to a third European Nations Cup success, Richie Dixon's appointment as the Lelos' head coach in mid-2010 came as a surprise. Prior to taking the role, Dixon, a former coach in his native Scotland, had been working for the IRB and as an adviser to the Georgia Rugby Union.

PLAYERS TO WATCH

1. **IRAKLI ABUSERIDZE** Age: 33; Position: scrum-half/captain; Club: Auxerre (Fra); Caps: 64; Points: 30 (6t)
2. **GEORGE CHKHAIDZE** Age: 28; Position: back row; Club: Montpellier-Hérault (Fra); Caps: 41; Points: 15 (3t)
3. **DAVID KACHARAVA** Age: 26; Position: centre; Club: Nice (Fra); Caps: 33; Points: 35 (7t)
4. **LASHA MALAGURADZE** Age: 25; Position: fly-half; Club: Béziers (Fra); Caps: 21; Points: 79 (3t, 11c, 11p, 3dg)
5. **MALKHAZ URJUKASHVILI** Age: 30; Position: full-back; Club: Gourdon (Fra); Caps: 64; Points: 295 (17t, 42c, 41p, 1dg)

Lelos lost their opening match against England (84–6), struggled to match Samoa's physicality (and lost 46–9), were overpowered by South Africa (and lost 46–19, although hooker David Dadunashvili did bag the consolation of scoring his country's first-ever try in the Tournament) and rounded out their first Rugby World Cup campaign with a disappointing 24–12 defeat to Uruguay – the one match they had a chance of winning. They had scored only one try in four matches and had leaked 200 points (an average of 50 per match): the message to Georgia was clear – there was still plenty of room for improvement.

Worryingly, Georgia suffered a post-Tournament slump in form, slipping to third place in the 2003–04 European Nations Cup and started their Rugby World Cup 2007 campaign with a disappointing 20–8 defeat to Romania in Bucharest. It was a painful defeat: with an automatic qualification place now out of reach, Georgia would have to secure a place in France the hard way. They kept their hopes alive with a 37–23 victory over Spain and progressed to Round 6 – a home-and-away tie against Portugal, with the winner gaining qualification and the loser progressing to a final repechage round. Georgia won 17–3 in Tbilisi, fought to a creditable 11–11 draw in Lisbon and celebrated the prospect of a second consecutive appearance on Rugby's grandest stage.

They performed with great credit in France, too: holding Argentina, the Tournament's form team, to a slender 6–3 half-time lead (before running out of steam and losing 33–3), coming within a whisker of shocking Ireland (only to lose an enthralling match 14–10) and recording their first-ever victory in the Tournament (scoring three tries en route to a 30–0 victory over Namibia) before bowing out of the Tournament following a tired 64–7 defeat to France. It had been a successful campaign and clear progress had been made.

Invigorated by their performances in France, Georgia have gone on to become the form team of second-tier European Rugby and regained the European Nations Cup in 2006–08 by winning nine of their ten matches. The prize in the 2008–10 edition of the competition was even greater: the Tournament served as Europe's Rugby World Cup 2011 qualifying group (with automatic places going to the winner and runner-up), so not only did Georgia have the chance to become the first team in 16 years to defend the title (since France in 1994), but a place in New Zealand was at stake. Georgia rose to the challenge in style: winning eight and drawing one of their ten matches to take the title. It was mission accomplished in a year that saw Rugby officially become Georgia's national sport. However, the Lelos have been placed in a tough group, alongside Argentina, England, Romania and Scotland and a victory against Romania is probably the best they can hope for.

Georgia's Rugby World Cup 2007 appearance was a success they will be looking to repeat.

Romania

Back in the early 1980s, following a series of high-profile victories, there was a growing clamour for Romania to join an expanded Five Nations Championship. Although only one of 12 teams to have played at all six Rugby World Cups, they are trying to regain that form.

RUGBY ROMANIA

The Oaks

www.rugby.ro

PLAYING STRIP
Yellow shirts, blue shorts, red socks

FORM SINCE RUGBY WORLD CUP 2007

Played:	27
Won:	17
Lost:	8
Drawn:	2
Winning percentage:	66.66
Points for:	731
Points against:	368
Points scored per match:	27.07
Points conceded per match:	13.63
Biggest victory:	76–7 v Czech Republic at Bucharest on 22 March 2008
Heaviest defeat:	22–7 v Georgia at Tbilisi on 9 February 2008

RUGBY WORLD CUP PERFORMANCES

1987	Group stage
1991	Group stage
1995	Group stage
1999	Group stage
2003	Group stage
2007	Group stage

Rugby was first brought to Romania around 1910 by students returning from Paris and, by 1913, the first clubs started to appear in Bucharest. But it wasn't until the late 1970s that Romania caused a stir in international Rugby.

Romania's communist regime saw the performance of its national teams as a propaganda tool and its players were given token jobs in the public sector that meant they could train together seven days a week in state-of-the-art facilities. In essence, this made them a forerunner to the teams of the modern professional era and, not surprisingly, the results started to show. In 1982, they beat France in Bucharest (13–9); they did the same to Wales in 1983 (24–6); and to Scotland a year later (28–22); and when they were invited to attend Rugby World Cup 1987, the Tournament provided them with the perfect platform to confirm their reputation as the fastest-improving team in world Rugby.

However, their performances in the competition fell short. They edged to victory over Zimbabwe in their opening game (21–20) and then crashed to defeats against both France (55–12) and Scotland (55–28). But then significant political events were to overtake the national team. December 1989 saw the overthrow of Nicolae Ceausescu's government and during the chaos captain Florica Murariu (who was also an army officer) was shot at a roadblock.

The fall of communism marked a new era for both Romania and its Rugby team: the state handouts disappeared, a significant number of players left the country to ply their trade in foreign leagues and the set-up that had served Romanian Rugby so well started to disintegrate, albeit slowly. They qualified comfortably for Rugby World Cup 1991 and although they lost their opening two matches – against France (30–3) and Canada (19–11) – departed the competition with their heads held high after recording a surprise 17–15 victory in their final game against Fiji. One win in three matches may not have been

what Romania had been hoping for going into the Tournament, but given what the national team had been over the previous two years, expectations on the team had been low.

They qualified for Rugby World Cup 1995 in South Africa with a 100 per cent record thanks to comfortable wins over Germany (60–6) and Russia (30–0), but found the going in the Tournament tough this time round and slumped to three disappointing, albeit hard-fought, defeats – against Canada (34–3), South Africa (21–8) and Australia (42–3). It remains Romania's worst-ever showing in the Tournament.

A pattern started to emerge: Romania had few problems qualifying for the

COACH

ROMEO GONTINEAC

A former centre who won 75 caps for his country, captained them on 14 occasions and is the only player in Romania's history to appear at four Rugby World Cups (1995–2007), Gontineac was part of the Oaks' coaching set-up for a year and a half before he was appointed as head coach in May 2010. He succeeded in his first task in the role – guiding his side through their Rugby World Cup qualification campaign to preserve Romania's record of having appeared in every Tournament – but greater challenges lie ahead for this legend.

STAR PLAYER

SORIN SOCOL

Position:	Lock/captain
Born:	30 November 1977, Bucharest, Romania
Club:	Lourdes (Fra)
Height:	1.96m (6ft 5in)
Weight:	110.7kg (244lb)
Caps:	55
Points:	40 (8t)

Socol was voted Player of the Tournament at the 1996 U21 Rugby World Championships but had to wait five years – during which time he played for French club Brive – before winning his first international cap (against Spain in 2001). He played in all four of Romania's matches at Rugby World Cup 2003 and became captain in February 2004. He led the Oaks during their unsuccessful 2007 campaign, but did not appear in a Romania shirt for 21 months. Recalled as captain to help Romania's faltering qualifying campaign for the 2011 Tournament, he is set to become only the fourth Romanian to appear in three Tournaments.

similar story at the 2007 Tournament: Romania won eight of their ten matches to claim the 2004–06 European Nations Cup (which served as Europe's initial qualifying Tournament) and a place in France only to record three defeats – against Italy (24–18), Scotland (42–0) and New Zealand (85–8) – and a solitary victory (14–10 against Portugal).

It wasn't until Romania tried to qualify for Rugby World Cup 2011, however, that their decline became truly apparent. A third-place finish at the 2008–10 European Nations Cup saw them miss out on the two available automatic qualifying spots, which left them facing a home-and-away tie against the Ukraine for the chance to progress to the final repechage round – they won 94–10 on aggregate.

Next up were Uruguay, with the winner taking the 20th and final spot at the 2011 Tournament: Romania drew 21–21 in Montevideo and won 39–12 in Bucharest to preserve their 100 per cent attendance record at the Tournament, but it had been a tough journey getting there. They will have low expectations going into the Tournament, with a victory over Georgia perhaps the best they can hope for, but don't be surprised if the Oaks lose all four of their matches and return home winless for the first time since 1995. These are tough times for Romanian Rugby.

Tournament but struggled once they got there. They won all four of their matches qualifying for the 1999 Tournament, but recorded only one victory in the Tournament itself (a slender 27–25 victory over the United States) to go with their two defeats – against Australia (57–9) and Ireland (44–14). A 67–6 qualifying victory over Spain proved enough to secure Romania a place at Rugby World Cup 2003, but yet again they struggled, reeling off three straight defeats – against Ireland (45–17), Australia (90–8) and Argentina (50–3) – before signing off with an expected victory over Namibia (37–7). It was a

Romania will be looking to progress beyond the Group stage for the first time in 2011.

PLAYERS TO WATCH

1. **IONUT DIMOFTE** Age: 26; Position: utility back; Club: Baia Mare (Rom); Caps: 48; Points: 66 (11t, 1c, 3p)
2. **CATALIN FERCU** Age: 24; Position: wing/centre; Club: Bucharest (Rom); Caps: 41; Points: 95 (19t)
3. **MARIUS TINCU** Age: 32; Position: hooker; Club: Perpignan (Fra); Caps: 41; Points: 70 (14t)
4. **OVIDIU TONITA** Age: 30; Position: flanker; Club: Perpignan (Fra); Caps: 52; Points: 65 (13t)
5. **FLORIN VLAICU** Age: 24; Position: utility back; Club: Bucharest (Rom); Caps: 34; Points: 178 (4t, 40c, 24p, 2dg)

WHEN SPORT AND POLITICS MET
24 JUNE 1995, ELLIS PARK, JOHANNESBURG

The enduring story of Rugby World Cup 1995 was how hosts South Africa, playing in the Tournament for the first time after apartheid-induced years in the sporting wilderness, grabbed first the attention and then the passionate support of an entire nation. It was a gradual process: when the Springboks topped their pool, the people of South Africa sat up and took notice; by the time they reached the Final, support had reached feverish levels; and when they saw off New Zealand in the final, a nation danced in the streets. And then came perhaps the most iconic image in sporting history: South Africa's new leader, Nelson Mandela, for so long the focal point of the anti-apartheid struggle, appeared on the podium wearing a Springbok shirt – a long-time symbol of Afrikaner power – to hand François Pienaar the Webb Ellis Cup. It was as profound a moment as sport can provide.

Nelson Mandela hands the Webb Ellis Cup to South African captain, François Pienaar.

Australia

New Zealand may have won more matches in the competition, but when it comes to claiming the ultimate prize, only South Africa can match Australia's pedigree at the Rugby World Cup. Today's young Wallabies carry a huge weight of expectation.

The great irony of what is undoubtedly Australia's remarkable Rugby World Cup success story is that the greatest side in their history never tasted Rugby World Cup glory. Having completed a memorable Grand Slam over the Home Nations countries in 1984 and a 2–1 away series win over New Zealand in 1986, Australia was considered hot favourite to win the first-ever Tournament. Everything seemed to be going according to plan when they beat England in their opening match (19–6), topped the pool and swept aside Ireland (33–15) in the quarter-finals. However, the dream came to a shuddering halt in the semi-finals: France's Serge Blanco scored a try in the dying moments of the game to hand his side a dramatic and memorable 30–24 victory.

The disappointment suffered in 1987 could only have added further fuel to Australia's sense of determination when they travelled to Europe for Rugby World Cup 1991. They opened with an impressive 32–19 win against Argentina and struggled to victory over Samoa (9–3) before hammering Wales (38–3) in Cardiff to win the group. Their smooth progress through the Tournament was almost derailed in their quarter-final match against Ireland in Dublin: the Wallabies trailed 18–15 with only seconds remaining when Michael Lynagh bundled his way over the line to secure a dramatic 19–18 victory. With their sense of destiny perhaps restored, they produced a scintillating first-half performance against New Zealand in the semi-final to take a 13–3 half-time lead and then hung on in the second half, showing they could combine defensive mettle to attacking flair, and won the day 16–6. It was a similar story in the final: Australia scored an early try, through Tony Daly, to establish a lead and then repelled wave after wave of England attacks to win the match 12–6. It was mission accomplished for Australia: they had become the champions of the world.

It was an ageing Australia squad that travelled to South Africa in 1995 and,

COACH

ROBBIE DEANS

Before he was appointed as Australia's first-ever foreign coach in December 2007, Robbie Deans was synonymous with New Zealand Rugby, first as a player (with Canterbury and the All Blacks) and then as a coach with Canterbury. And although his focus on developing a young Wallaby side did not produce immediate success – Australia finished second in the 2008 Tri-Nations and third the following year – by 2010, clear progress had been made. Although a Kiwi Deans would like nothing more than for Australia to shatter the All Blacks' dream of winning Rugby World Cup 2011 on home soil.

Wallabies
www.rugby.com.au

PLAYING STRIP Gold shirts with green trim, green shorts, green socks

FORM SINCE RUGBY WORLD CUP 2007

Played:	43
Won:	24
Lost:	18
Drawn:	1
Winning percentage:	56.97
Points for:	1,047
Points against:	883
Points scored per match:	24.35
Points conceded per match:	20.53
Biggest victory:	49–3 v Fiji at Canberra on 5 June 2010
Heaviest defeat:	53–8 v South Africa at Johannesburg on 30 August 2008

RUGBY WORLD CUP PERFORMANCES

1987	Semi-finals
1991	WORLD CHAMPIONS
1995	Quarter-finals
1999	WORLD CHAMPIONS
2003	Runners-up
2007	Quarter-finals

from the moment they lost their opening match against the Springboks (27–18), it was clear that this was a collection of players whose glory days were behind them. They beat Canada (27–11) and Romania (42–3) to qualify for the quarter-finals, but then lost to England (25–22) in a thrilling match in Cape Town. Defeat marked the end of an era and the Rugby World Cup had seen the last of Michael Lynagh and his team.

And so it was a new generation of Wallabies that descended on the northern hemisphere for Rugby World Cup 1999– in a squad few thought capable of winning the Tournament. They eased through their group in impressive fashion, cruising to

STAR PLAYER

DAVID POCOCK

Position: ....Flanker
Born: .... 23 April 1988, Messina, Zimbabwe
Club: .... Western Force (Aus)
Height: 1.83m (6ft)
Weight: 102.5kg (226lb)
Caps: 30
Points: 10 (2t)

David Pocock made his international debut against New Zealand in November 2008. But it was in 2009 that Pocock, a foraging openside flanker, showed his real worth to the Wallabies: he played 13 out of 14 internationals that year and, with his speed around the pitch and his supreme ability at the breakdown, provided the forward link Australia's exciting backline required to play a more expansive game. His good form continued into 2010: he played a starring role in Australia's victory over South Africa in Brisbane, cemented his place in the Wallabies' line-up and ended the season being voted his country's Player of the Year.

comfortable wins over Romania (57–9), Ireland (23–3) and the United States (55–19), beat Wales (24–9) in a one-sided quarter-final in Cardiff and edged past South Africa (27–21) in a tense semi-final at Twickenham. In what seemed like the blink of an eye, the team no one had expected to win had marched serenely to the Final, where they would face France (unexpected

conquerors of New Zealand in the other semi-final). Australia scored two tries to France's none and won the most one-sided Rugby World Cup Final in history (35–12) to become world champions for a second time.

Four years later, as Tournament hosts, they came mighty close to becoming the first team in history to defend their world crown. They started out

with leisurely wins against Argentina (24–8) and Romania (90–8), produced a stunning 22-try demolition of Namibia to win 142–0 (the most tries scored by a team and the largest winning margin in the Tournament's history) and then scrambled past Ireland (17–16) to win the group. They beat Scotland in the quarter-finals (33–16) and then produced their best performance of the Tournament to shock New Zealand in the semi-finals (22–10) only to be undone by a dominant England pack and the boot of Jonny Wilkinson in the Final.

Home victories over New Zealand (20–15) and South Africa (25–17) in the build-up to Rugby World Cup 2007 suggested that Australia would be a major contender for the title yet again, but it wasn't to be: after winning their group comfortably they came unstuck in the quarter-finals against an inspired England pack and lost 12–10.

Since then, the Wallabies, under coach Robbie Deans, have introduced young talent into the line-up (such as Quade Cooper and James O'Connor), have developed arguably the most exciting backline in world Rugby and, crucially, have sought to address the problems in the pack that have undermined their last two Rugby World Cup campaigns. As is always the case, by the time the Wallabies arrive in New Zealand they will be major contenders for the title.

The class of 2007 have given way to a revamped team who are contenders for the 2011 title.

PLAYERS TO WATCH

1. **QUADE COOPER** Age: 22; Position: fly-half; Club: Queensland Reds (Aus); Caps: 24; Points: 41 (6t, 1c, 3p)
2. **ROCKY ELSOM** Age: 27; Position: flanker/captain; Club: Brumbies (Aus); Caps: 64; Points: 60 (12t)
3. **WILL GENIA** Age: 23; Position: scrum-half; Club: Queensland Reds (Aus); Caps: 22; Points: 20 (4t)
4. **MATT GITEAU** Age: 28; Position: inside-centre; Club: Brumbies (Aus); Caps: 91; Points: 666 (28t, 101c, 104p, 4dg)
5. **JAMES O'CONNOR** Age: 20; Position: wing/full-back; Club: Western Force (Aus); Caps: 27; Points: 119 (10t, 18c, 11p)

Ireland

Ireland are one of the world's most consistent Test nations and although Rugby World Cup 2007 was disappointing for a golden generation of players seeking to win the Tournament, they will be trying to capture their best form this time around.

Ireland could have had few expectations of winning Rugby World Cup in 1987. After winning two Triple Crowns in five years (in 1982 and 1985), Ireland had won only two of their last eight matches in the Five Nations Championship. They duly lost their opening match to Wales (13–6), beating Canada (46–19) and Tonga (32–9) to finish as group runners-up, but then proving no match for Australia in the quarter-finals and losing the match 33–15.

It was a familiar tale four years later. All the good work achieved with opening victories over Zimbabwe (55–11) and Japan (32–16) was undone when they lost their final pool match to Scotland at Murrayfield (24–15). Defeat left them as pool runners-up and, as had been the case four years earlier, condemned the Irish to a quarter-final clash against Australia. They fared much better this time round and, as the Game entered its dying moments, Ireland held a slender 18–15 lead and, with it, dreams of reaching the semi-finals. However Australia's Michael Lynagh forced his way over the line to score a famous 19–18 Wallabies victory. The lesson for Ireland was clear: win your group.

Hopes of doing so were dashed when Ireland opened their Rugby World Cup 1995 campaign with a 43–19 defeat to New Zealand. They rallied well to beat Japan (50–28) to set up a final pool-match showdown against Wales, with the losers of the match facing elimination from the Tournament: Ireland scored three tries to Wales' two and won 24–23. Their reward was a quarter-final against France, who proved too strong and cruised to a 36–12 win. Ireland had crashed out at the last-eight stage for the third Tournament in a row; that would change in 1999 – and not for the better. An alteration to the format at Rugby World Cup 1999 meant that Ireland's second-place group finish would see them play Argentina in a quarter-final playoff match. To

COACH

DECLAN KIDNEY

In May 2008, following disappointing Rugby World Cup 2007 and 2008 Six Nations campaigns, the Ireland RFU decided to replace Eddie O'Sullivan as coach and turned to Declan Kidney as the man to revive Ireland's waning fortunes. Kidney, who as coach had led Ireland U19 to FIRA World Cup glory in 1998 and Munster to four Heineken Cup finals (and to victory in 2006 and 2008) did a fantastic job, guiding Ireland to their first Grand Slam in 61 years in his first year in charge and ending the season as the IRB Coach of the Year In association with Emirates Airline.

the surprise of many, the Pumas edged a tense match in Lens 28–24 and Ireland had failed to reach the last eight for the first time in their history.

The poor campaign marked a turning point in Irish Rugby. The foundation of the Celtic League in 2001 meant that Ireland's leading players – usually plying their trade overseas in their quest for top-flight Rugby – returned to Ireland in droves. As a result, Ireland's international players started to play with and against each other on a regular basis and the main beneficiary was the national team.

The results started to show: they finished second in the 2001 Six Nations, repeated the performance in 2003 and

Ireland
www.irishrugby.ie

PLAYING STRIP Green shirts with white trim, white shorts, green socks

FORM SINCE RUGBY WORLD CUP 2007

Played:	31
Won:	18
Lost:	12
Drawn:	1
Winning percentage:	59.67
Points for:	677
Points against:	551
Points scored per match:	21.84
Points conceded per match:	17.77
Biggest victory:	55–0 v Canada at Limerick on 8 November 2008
Heaviest defeat:	66–28 v New Zealand at New Plymouth on 12 June 2010

RUGBY WORLD CUP PERFORMANCES

1987	Quarter-finals
1991	Quarter-finals
1995	Quarter-finals
1999	Quarter-final playoffs
2003	Quarter-finals
2007	Group stages

STAR PLAYER

JAMIE HEASLIP

Position:	No. 8
Born:	15 December 1983, Tiberias, Israel
Club:	Leinster (Ire)
Height:	1.92m (6ft 3in)
Weight:	108.4kg (239lb)
Caps:	31
Points:	25 (5t)

A standout performer for Ireland U21s, Jamie Heaslip broke into the Leinster side in 2004–05 and made his debut for Ireland against the Pacific Islanders in November 2006. He missed out on Rugby World Cup 2007, but appeared in four of Ireland's 2008 Six Nations matches and, in 2009, having finally made the No. 8 jersey his own, came to the fore, scoring tries against France and Scotland as Ireland claimed their first Grand Slam for 61 years. He then won the Heineken Cup with Leinster and played in all three tests against South Africa for the British & Irish Lions. By 2010, he was being hailed as the best No. 8 in European Rugby.

Ronan O'Gara had developed into a serial points accumulator; their pack was starting to show it had the physical grunt to compete with the very best; they had won three Six Nations Triple Crowns in four years; and they had recorded significant home victories over Australia and South Africa. The weight of expectation got to them: despite winning their opening two games – against Namibia (32–17) and Georgia (14–10) – they performed poorly in both matches and then slumped to defeats against France (25–3) and Argentina (30–15) to crash out of the Tournament at the group stages for the first time in their history.

But it was only after Ireland's poor showing in the 2008 Six Nations (in which they won only two of their five matches) that a new direction was sought. Out went coach Eddie O'Sullivan, in came Declan Kidney (who had led Munster to two Heineken Cup victories) and the change was immediate: in 2009, Ireland won the Grand Slam for the first time in 61 years. The good form has not continued, however: they lost twice in the 2010 Six Nations and then slumped to successive defeats against New Zealand (twice), Australia and South Africa. Ireland, though, are a talented side, capable of beating anyone on their day, and they will be looking to progress beyond the quarter-finals.

travelled to that year's Rugby World Cup in great shape. They opened their campaign with victories over Romania (45–17) and Namibia (64–7) and edged to a 16–15 victory over Argentina to set up a final pool match against hosts Australia. The match carried a significant prize for the winner: top spot in the group. The Wallabies won 17–16 and yet again Ireland's failure to win the group proved costly: they faced France in the quarter-finals and fell to a disappointing 43–21 defeat.

Pundits thought Ireland had a real chance at Rugby World Cup 2007: the team had been together for some time; they had performed well at the previous Tournament; their captain, Brian O'Driscoll, had cemented a reputation as the best centre in world Rugby;

Ireland's talented team needs to move up a gear if they are to truly shine in 2011.

PLAYERS TO WATCH

1. **TOMMY BOWE** Age: 26; Position: winger; Club: Ospreys (Wal); Caps: 36; Points: 80 (16t)
2. **STEPHEN FERRIS** Age: 25; Position: flanker/No. 8; Club: Ulster (Ire); Caps: 24; Points: 10 (2t)
3. **BRIAN O'DRISCOLL** Age: 32; Position: outside-centre/captain; Club: Leinster (Ire); Caps: 107; Points: 220 (41t, 5dg)
4. **PAUL O'CONNELL** Age: 31; Position: lock; Club: Munster (Ire); Caps: 70; Points: 30 (6t)
5. **DAVID WALLACE** Age: 34; Position: flanker; Club: Munster (Ire); Caps: 66; Points: 60 (12t)

Italy

Proud members of the Six Nations Championship since 2000 and a participant at every one of the six Rugby World Cups, Italy's record in the Tournament is strong but they are still waiting to regularly beat the world's best teams.

The Azzurri
www.federugby.it

PLAYING STRIP Light blue shirts, white shorts, light blue socks

FORM SINCE RUGBY WORLD CUP 2007

Played:	31
Won:	5
Lost:	26
Drawn:	0
Winning percentage:	16.12
Points for:	400
Points against:	857
Points scored per match:	12.90
Points conceded per match:	27.65
Biggest victory:	24–6 v Samoa
at Ascoli on 28 November 2009	
Heaviest defeat:	55–11 v South Africa
at East London on 26 June 2010	

RUGBY WORLD CUP PERFORMANCES

1987	Group stages
1991	Group stages
1995	Group stages
1999	Group stages
2003	Group stages
2007	Group stages

Italy were given one of the 16 invitations to play in the inaugural Rugby World Cup in 1987. The Tournament gave them a chance to display their talent on the biggest possible stage and provided them with a platform to further their cause for inclusion among Europe's Rugby elite. They were handed the toughest of starts when drawn to play against co-hosts New Zealand in the opening match of the Tournament at Eden Park, Auckland, and capitulated to a 70–6 defeat. The Azzurri performed better in a losing cause against Argentina, but the 25–16 defeat to the Pumas rendered their final pool-match victory over Fiji (18–15) meaningless – Italy had finished bottom of their pool.

They were drawn in a tough group for the second successive Tournament in 1991, alongside New Zealand (again), England and the United States. They won their opening match, as expected, against the Americans (30–9) and although they lost against New Zealand (31–21) and England (36–6), their gritty performances in both matches suggested that progress had been made.

It was more of the same at Rugby World Cup 1995 in South Africa. After losing their opening match in disappointing fashion to Samoa (42–18), a game many had expected them to win, they pushed England all the way in their second match (only to lose out 27–20) and carried that form into their final pool match against Argentina, which they won 31–25. Italy had again failed to progress beyond the group stages, but it was clear that Italian Rugby had matured and that they had found a way of competing with the best teams in world Rugby.

All of which made Italy's performance at Rugby World Cup 1999 disappointing. In the four years building up to the Tournament, the Azzurri had recorded wins over France and Ireland, had pushed England hard in a Rugby World Cup qualifying match (only to lose a game they should have won 23–15) and, most importantly of all, had won their battle for inclusion in an expanded Five Nations Championship (starting from 2000). If the Tournament represented a chance for Italy to prove they were worthy of such an elevation in status, they fell apart, losing heavily to England (67–7), narrowly to Tonga (28–25) and very heavily again to New Zealand (101–3). It was the first time in their history that Italy had failed to win a match at a Rugby World Cup.

These were challenging times for Italian Rugby. Rugby World Cup 1999 disaster had shown that the core of players who had pushed Italy into the international Rugby limelight, and the

COACH

NICK MALLETT

A former player with Western Province and South Africa, Nick Mallett cut his coaching teeth in French club Rugby and back in South Africa with the Boland Cavaliers before becoming South Africa's assistant coach in 1996 and head coach the following year. He got off to a great start, leading the Springboks to a world record-equalling 17 consecutive victories, but they had peaked too soon and, following a disappointing Rugby World Cup 1999 campaign, he resigned in 2000. After spells with Stade Français and Western Province, he took over from Pierre Berbizier as Italy's head coach in 2007.

STAR PLAYER

SERGIO PARISSE

Position: ....No. 8/captain
Born: . 12 September 1983, La Plata, Argentina
Club: ....Stade Français (Fra)
Height: 1.96m (6ft 5in)
Weight: 105.7kg (233lb)
Caps: 72
Points: 28 (5t, 1dg)

Sergio Parisse made his debut (aged 18) against New Zealand at Hamilton in June 2002 and scored his first international try against Canada at Rugby World Cup 2003. With his great positional sense in the lineout, innate ability to read the Game in defence and gain the hard yards in attack, he is one of the best No. 8s in world Rugby. He was Italy's best player at Rugby World Cup 2007 and continued his form into 2008 – during which he became captain – and ended the year among the nominees for the IRB Player of the Year award. He missed Italy's 2010 Six Nations campaign with a serious knee injury, but expects to be back in 2011.

won the match (27–15) and the Azzurri, although they had won twice, were the only Six Nations team not to advance to the last eight.

Rugby World Cup 2007 provided onlookers with a similar sense of déjà vu. Italy opened their campaign with a 76–14 defeat to New Zealand – remarkably the fifth time the Italians had been drawn in the same group as the All Blacks in six Tournaments – but then beat Romania (24–18) and Portugal (31–5) to set up a showdown with Scotland (a team they had beaten, at Murrayfield, in the Six Nations that year) for the runners-up spot in the pool and a place in the quarter-finals. This time they lost 18–16 and this defeat was the hardest to take for Italy.

There is no simple solution to Italy's inability to push through to the next level – although they have used five coaches in the last decade trying to find one. The issue is as follows: whereas the Azzurri's pack has been consistently good enough to take the attack to any opponent, their back division lacks the incisiveness to take full advantage of the situations they find themselves in. Such an imbalance makes regular victories over world Rugby's best teams a difficult proposition for Italy, and it's hard to see that pattern changing at Rugby World Cup 2011.

Italy's star players will need to lead from the front if the team is to realise its full potential.

ones who had presented such a strong case for inclusion in the Six Nations Championship, was coming to the end of the line. The timing could not have been worse. Italy started to rebuild their team in the full glare of the Six Nations spotlight, finished bottom in their first three campaigns and, in 2003, finished fifth. It gave them little confidence going into the 2003 Rugby World Cup.

They lost their opening match against New Zealand (70–7) but responded well, beating Tonga (36–12) and Canada (19–14) – the first time Italy had won back-to-back matches in the Tournament – to set up a final-match showdown against Wales (a team they had beaten in the Six Nations Championship only months earlier) for the pool's last quarter-final slot. Wales

PLAYERS TO WATCH

1. **MAURO BERGAMASCO** Age: 31; Position: flanker; Club: Stade Français (Fra); Caps: 84; Points: 70 (14t)
2. **MIRCO BERGAMASCO** Age: 27; Position: wing/centre; Club: Racing Métro (Fra); Caps: 76; Points: 189 (17t, 7c, 30p)
3. **MARTÍN CASTROGIOVANNI** Age: 29; Position: prop; Club: Leicester Tigers (Eng); Caps: 71; Points: 50 (10t)
4. **LUKE McLEAN** Age: 23; Position: full-back; Club: Benetton Treviso (Ita); Caps: 24; Points: 49 (2t, 13p)
5. **FABIO ONGARO** Age: 33; Position: hooker; Club: Aironi (Ita); Caps: 74; Points: 20 (4t)

Russia

Russia is one of the sleeping giants of world Rugby. In 2010, the giant finally opened its eyes: when Russia finished second in the 2008–10 European Nations Cup, they secured Rugby World Cup qualification for the first time in their history.

Reputedly, a French journalist introduced Rugby to Russia in the early 1920s and a national championship was formed. However, during the 1940s Stalin labelled Rugby a hobby for capitalists and banned it. A thaw started in 1957 and although the matches aroused great interest at the time, the pick-up of the Game in the country (where football and ice hockey dominated) continued to be slow.

COACH

NIKOLAY NERUSH

An established and respected coach in Russian domestic Rugby, Nikolay Nerush is the head coach of VVA-Podmoskovye Monino, the dominant force in Russian Rugby who have won the last five national championships and who provide the vast majority of players to the national team. He replaced the experienced Claude Saurel as Russia's head coach in August 2008 and got off to a blistering start with the national team, guiding them to second place at the 2008–10 European Nations Cup and, with it, securing his country a place at the Rugby World Cup for the first time in their history.

The Soviet Union made their first appearance on the international stage in 1975 at the FIRA Trophy, a forerunner to today's European Nations Cup. Their performances in the competition throughout the 1970s and 1980s were encouraging enough to receive an invitation to appear at the inaugural Rugby World Cup in 1987 – an invite they declined on political grounds. The collapse of the Soviet Union in 1991 unfortunately also set back Rugby development in the country.

International Rugby was played under a Commonwealth of Independent States flag between 1991 and 1992 (the team lost all four of the matches it played) and for the first time under a Russia flag on 6 June 1992, against the Barbarians – a match they won 27–23. The national side, under its new guise, then embarked on a five-match unbeaten run – still the longest in the country's history – before losing to Italy in Moscow (30–19).

The biggest test, however, was still to come. In 1994, Russia attempted to qualify for the Rugby World Cup for the first time. They started well, recording wins over Georgia (15–9) and Poland (41–5) to progress to the second stage, a round-robin group against Germany and Romania. They completed a comprehensive victory over Germany (60–6) before crashing to defeat against Romania (30–0) and Russia's Rugby World Cup dreams were over. They tried again four years later, but lost three of their four matches – against Croatia (23–16), Italy (48–18) and Georgia (12–6) – which rendered their 45–9

Russia
www.rugby.ru

PLAYING STRIP
White shirts, white shorts, white socks

FORM SINCE RUGBY WORLD CUP 2007

Played:	24
Won:	15
Lost:	8
Drawn:	1
Winning percentage:	64.58
Points for:	628
Points against:	490
Points scored per match:	24.17
Points conceded per match:	20.42
Biggest victory:	53–0 v Germany
	at Hanover on 2 May 2009
Heaviest defeat:	75–3 v Japan
	at Tokyo on 6 November 2010

RUGBY WORLD CUP PERFORMANCES

1987	Did not enter
1991	Did not enter
1995	Did not qualify
1999	Did not qualify
2003	Did not qualify
2007	Did not qualify

victory over Denmark meaningless. Russia were struggling to find a foothold.

By 2003, however, many thought that Russia, who had finished third in their previous two European Nations Cup campaigns, stood their best chance yet of qualifying for the Rugby World Cup. They started their campaign impressively, recording victories over the Czech Republic (37–8) and the Netherlands (65–3) to progress to Round 5 and although they lost both matches in the round-robin group – to Ireland (35–3) and Georgia (17–3) – their dream wasn't over. Qualification now rested on a winner-takes-all, home-and-away repechage tie against Spain. They won 36–3 in Madrid, lost 38–22 at home

STAR PLAYER

YURIY KUSHNAREV

Position:	Fly-half/full-back
Born:	6 June 1985
Club:	VVA-Podmoskovye Monino
Height:	1.83m (6ft)
Weight:	95kg (209lb)
Caps:	34
Points:	238 (6t, 29c, 50p)

A member of the VVA-Podmoskovye team, Yuriy Kushnarev made his international debut against Georgia in February 2006 and has been a constant presence in Russia's line-up ever since. He showed his value during the 2008–10 European Nations Cup, which also served as an initial qualifying phase for Rugby World Cup 2011. Kushnarev scored 15 points during Russia's 42–15 opening victory over Spain, ten in their crucial 28–19 away victory over Romania and 11 during the 21–21 home draw with Romania that ensured Russia qualified for 2011. Kushnarev had scored 105 of Russia's 291 points during the campaign – a critical contribution.

in Krasnodar and won the biggest contest in their Rugby history 58–41 on aggregate. If only the story had stopped there: six weeks later, news emerged that Russia's Rugby authorities had failed to provide the proof of three of their players' eligibility – South Africa-born trio Johan Hendriks, Renier Volschenk and Werner Pieterse – and that they had been ejected from the competition, with Spain taking their place. Russia's Rugby World Cup dreams ended there for that Tournament.

A fourth-place finish in the 2003–04 European Nations Cup suggested that

Russia were in good shape by the time the 2004–06 European Nations Cup campaign came around, and this time the Tournament came with an added twist: it would also serve as Europe's Rugby World Cup 2007 qualifying Tournament, with two automatic places going to the top two teams. Russia finished fourth. They kept their hopes alive with a 62–28 aggregate victory over the Ukraine, but then lost both of the Round 5 matches – against Italy (67–7) and Portugal (26–23) – to miss out yet again. It was yet another case of what could have been.

Many sides would have faltered had they suffered a similar succession of disappointments, but, to their great credit, Russia bounced back stronger. They finished second in the 2006–08 European Nations Cup and entered the 2008–10 edition of the Tournament (which would serve as the initial phase of European qualifying for Rugby World Cup 2011) in high hopes. They won seven and drew one of their ten matches to finish second. The journey may have been a long one, but Russia had finally earned their place on Rugby's biggest stage. And all eyes will be on them when they get there. Victories over bigger teams such as Australia, Ireland and Italy may need to be very hard won, but expect them to put up a fight in their match against the United States – the two countries have met on four previous occasions and are level on wins with two apiece.

PLAYERS TO WATCH

1. **ALEXANDER GVOZDOVSKY** Age: 30; Position: wing; Club: Krasny Yar (Rus); Caps: 31; Points: 75 (15t)
2. **ALEXANDER KHROHIN** Age: 34; Position: prop; Club: VVA-Podmoskovye (Rus); Caps: 66; Points: 40 (8t)
3. **VLADISLAV KORSHUNOV** Age: 27; Position: hooker/captain; Club: VVA-Podmoskovye (Rus); Caps: 47; Points: 20 (4t)
4. **SERGEY TRISHIN** Age: 26; Position: centre; Club: VVA-Podmoskovye (Rus); Caps: 32; Points: 25 (5t)
5. **ALEXANDER YANYUSHKIN** Age: 28; Position: scrum-half/fly-half; Club: VVA-Podmoskovye (Rus); Caps: 40; Points: 103 (8t, 9c, 15p)

Russia have finally made it to Rugby World Cup – their participation has been long overdue.

USA

In the USA, interest in Rugby lags a long way behind American football, baseball, basketball and ice hockey. Amazing, then, that the United States national Rugby team has made it to six of the seven Rugby World Cups.

Rugby is an established minority sport in the United States, albeit one with a rich history. By the 1870s, British immigrants set up a thriving Rugby scene in San Francisco and by 1912, the national team had played its first international – a 12–8 defeat to Australia.

It seemed a promise of great things when the United States struck Rugby gold at the 1920 Olympic Games in Antwerp, shocking France in the final (8–0). That was enhanced when they

defended their title in Paris four years later, again against France. Soon afterwards, however, the International Olympic Committee removed Rugby from the Games and interest in Rugby in the United States waned. The national team did not contest another fixture for 52 years, and the Game became the preserve of immigrants or students at colleges with a Rugby tradition.

The sport enjoyed something of a renaissance in the 1960s and early 1970s, leading in 1975 to the foundation of a governing body, USA Rugby. The national team reappeared in 1976 with a 24–12 defeat to Australia and, despite indifferent performances (they had won only four of 22 matches in 11 years), the United States was invited to Rugby World Cup 1987. The Eagles travelled to Australia more in hope than expectation and got off to a blistering start, beating Japan in their opening game (21–18) before slumping to defeats against Australia (47–12) and England (34–6).

The Eagles lost three of their four qualifiers for Rugby World Cup 1991 in a group containing Canada and Argentina, but, given that the matches were played only to seed the teams, rather than to eliminate them, it meant that the defeats were not as damaging as perhaps they should have been. Instead, it showed that the Eagles were in no form going into their second Rugby World Cup and that was confirmed when, in the Tournament itself,

they went on to lose all three matches – against Italy (30–9), New Zealand (46–6) and England (37–9).

If the qualifying set-up for Rugby World Cup 1991 had helped the United States, the revamped qualifiers for the 1995 Tournament hindered them: only one spot was made available for the entire Americas section. The Eagles beat Bermuda (60–3) to win the continent's north section and then played Argentina, a country with considerably more international Rugby pedigree: they lost 28–22 at home and 16–11 away and missed out on the fun in South Africa.

A change in the qualifying Tournament for the third successive Tournament left the United States needing to win

COACH

EDDIE O'SULLIVAN

Eddie O'Sullivan made his name as a top-class coach in his native Ireland, first with Blackrock College and Connacht, then with Ireland U21 (who he led to a Triple Crown in 1996) and, finally, between 2002 and 2008, with the Ireland national team, who won three Triple Crowns and rose to third in the IRB World Rankings under his charge. He quit in March 2008, following Ireland's disappointing Rugby World Cup 2007 and 2008 Six Nations campaigns, and, seeking to restore his reputation, accepted the post of United States' head coach in September 2009.

The Eagles
www.usarugby.org

PLAYING STRIP White shirts with red and blue trim, white shorts, blue socks

FORM SINCE RUGBY WORLD CUP 2007

Played:	14
Won:	7
Lost:	7
Drawn:	0
Winning percentage:	50.00
Points for:	307
Points against:	427
Points scored per match:	21.93
Points conceded per match:	26.69
Biggest victory:	43–9 v Uruguay in Salt Lake City on 8 November 2008
Heaviest defeat:	48–15 v Wales in Chicago on 6 June 2009

RUGBY WORLD CUP PERFORMANCES

1987	Group stages
1991	Group stages
1995	Did not qualify
1999	Group stages
2003	Group stages
2007	Group stages

STAR PLAYER

TODD CLEVER

Position: ....No. 8/captain
Born: 16 January 1983, Palm Springs, Ca, USA
Club: ....Suntory Sungoliath (Jap)
Height: 1.93m (6ft 4in)
Weight: 96.6kg (213lb)
Caps: 33
Points: 40 (8t)

Todd Clever first played Rugby at high school, turned out for the United States U19s in 2000, then made his international debut against Argentina in August 2003 – though he had to wait two years for his second cap. After spending 2006 with North Harbour in New Zealand (one of the toughest leagues in the world), he was selected for Rugby World Cup 2007 and played in all four matches. Appointed captain of the national side in 2008, he signed for Lions in South Africa in 2009 and went on to become the first American to play in the Super 14, and the first to score a try in the competition. He moved to Suntory in Japan for 2010.

at least one of their group matches (against Argentina, Canada and Uruguay) to secure a place at Rugby World Cup 1999: they lost to Argentina (52–24) and Canada (31–14) before edging to a 21–16 victory over Uruguay. The Eagles fared little better at the Tournament proper, however, again losing all three of their matches – against Ireland (53–8), Romania (27–25) and Australia (55–19).

Defeats to Canada and Uruguay in the Americas qualifying section for Rugby World Cup 2003 left the United States facing a potentially tricky final repechage against Spain (who had made their debut at the Tournament in 1999), but the Eagles proved too strong for the Spanish, winning 62–13 in Madrid and 58–13 back home to secure a comfortable 120–26 aggregate

victory. They performed better at the Tournament itself too, losing narrowly to Fiji (19–18) and creditably to Scotland (39–15) before beating Japan (39–26) for their first win in the competition for 16 years. They may have lost 41–14 to France in the final pool match, but Rugby World Cup 2003 had given American Rugby some cause for cheer.

The story of the United States' qualification for Rugby World Cup 2007 was a familiar one: despite losing to Canada (56–7) in their opening qualifying group, an earlier victory over Barbados (69–3) was enough to secure a second chance: a home-and-away tie against Uruguay, with the winner securing a berth in France: the Eagles won the tie 75–20 on aggregate. Placed in a tough group, they performed with great credit but still lost all four matches – against England (28–10), Tonga (25–15), Samoa (25–21) and South Africa (64–15).

The pattern seems to have been set for American Rugby at the Rugby World Cup and buoyed by the Rugby Sevens inclusion in the Olympics expect the Game to grow rapidly over the next five years. A victory over Russia will be the Eagles' minimum requirement at the 2011 Tournament, but it would be a major surprise if the United States achieve anything more than that.

The United States have shown that they can qualify well but now need Rugby World Cup wins.

PLAYERS TO WATCH

1. **PAUL EMERICK** Age: 31; Position: utility back; Club: Ulster (Ire); Caps: 39; Points: 60 (12t)
2. **TAKU NGWENYA** Age: 25; Position: wing; Club: Biarritz (Fra); Caps: 17; Points: 35 (7t)
3. **TIM USASZ** Age: 27; Position: scrum-half; Club: Nottingham (Eng); Caps: 10; Points: 10 (2t)
4. **JOHN VAN DER GEISSEN** Age: 28; Position: lock; Club: Bath (Eng); Caps: 14; Points: 5 (1t)
5. **CHRIS WYLES** Age: 27; Position: full-back/wing; Club: Saracens (Eng); Caps: 23; Points: 28 (5t, 1dg)

THE GREATEST GAME IN RUGBY WORLD CUP HISTORY
31 OCTOBER 1999, TWICKENHAM, LONDON

At 24–10, it seemed as though pre-Tournament favourites New Zealand were set to breeze past France in the second of the Rugby World Cup 1999 semi-finals at Twickenham. But the French – written off as no-hopers before the match – had other ideas. Spurred on by fly-half Christophe Lamaison, who scored two penalties and two drop-goals in quick succession, Les Bleus roared back into contention (24–22) and then left the reeling All Blacks in their wake, scoring three unanswered tries – through Christophe Dominici, Richard Dourthe and Philippe Bernat-Salles – to surge into a 43–24 lead. Jeff Wilson scored a late consolation try for New Zealand, but when the final whistle went, France had won the match 43–31 and had completed the most remarkable comeback in the Tournament's history.

French players celebrate their shock comeback to reach the Rugby World Cup 1999 Final.

South Africa

A nation with both a passion for and a proud history in the Game, Rugby World Cup has provided South Africa with two of their greatest moments on a Rugby pitch: their ecstatic 1995 win on home soil and their 2007 win over England.

Springboks
www.sarugby.net

PLAYING STRIP Green shirts with gold collar, white shorts, green socks

FORM SINCE RUGBY WORLD CUP 2007

Played:	40
Won:	26
Lost:	14
Drawn:	0
Winning percentage:	65.00
Points for:	1,067
Points against:	800
Points scored per match:	26.68
Points conceded per match:	20.00
Biggest victory:	63–9 v Argentina at Johannesburg on 9 August 2008
Heaviest defeat:	32–12 v New Zealand at Auckland on 10 July 2010

RUGBY WORLD CUP PERFORMANCES

1987	Did not enter
1991	Did not enter
1995	WORLD CHAMPIONS
1999	Semi-finals
2003	Quarter-finals
2007	WORLD CHAMPIONS

South Africa were non-participants at the first two Rugby World Cups (in 1987 and 1991) as a result of apartheid, but by 1992 the political sands were shifting: Nelson Mandela had been released; a new, truly representative government was about to take power; the South Africa national team had been welcomed back into the international Rugby fold; and, what's more, the IRB had awarded them hosting rights for Rugby World Cup 1995. Such explosive ingredients would provide one of those rare moments when sport and politics dovetail to extraordinary effect.

It would be wrong to suggest that the entire South African nation was behind the national team – the Springboks, after all, were a powerful symbol of the old Afrikaner era. This was more of a slow-burning love affair, but it was one that got off to an electrifying start.

South Africa's first test in the Rugby World Cup was a daunting one: a Tournament-opening match against defending champions Australia. They won (27–18) and, from that moment on, belief began to grow both inside and outside the camp. That growth continued with comfortable, if not quite convincing, victories over Romania (21–8) and Canada (20–0) and turned into clamour when they beat Samoa (42–15) in the quarter-finals, with Chester Williams – the only black player in the squad – scoring four of the Springboks' six tries.

They got slightly lucky against France in the semi-finals, when a saturated Durban pitch reduced what could have been a tough test into a soggy, forward battle that suited them down to the ground, and won the error-strewn match 19–15. They needed little luck in the final against New Zealand though, as they out-muscled the All Blacks to win 15–12 in extra-time, with Joel Stransky kicking all of his team's points. The sight of Nelson Mandela,

wearing a replica No. 6 Springbok shirt, handing South Africa captain François Pienaar the Webb Ellis Cup is one of the most iconic images in sporting history.

After the hysteria of 1995, Rugby World Cup 1999 was always going to be something of an anticlimax, but South Africa made a commendable defence of their crown. They eased to top spot in their pool, cruising to victories over Scotland (46–19), Spain (47–3) and Uruguay (39–3) and brushed aside the attentions of England (44–21) in the quarter-final, with fly-half Jannie de Beer nailing a Tournament-record five drop-goals. But the journey ended in defeat to Australia (27–21) in the semi-final.

COACH

PETER DE VILLIERS

When Peter de Villiers took over as South Africa coach in January 2008 he inherited a team in transition and with several stars playing abroad after the Rugby World Cup 2007 success. South Africa finished bottom in the 2008 Tri-Nations but de Villiers' team responded well in 2009, recording a series victory over the British & Irish Lions and claiming their third Tri-Nations crown. With victories in November 2010 against Ireland and England It appears South Africa is timing its resurgence perfectly ahead of its Rugby World Cup title defence.

STAR PLAYER

MORNÉ STEYN

Position: ....Fly-half
Born: ....11 July 1984, Belleville, South Africa
Club: ....Blue Bulls (SA)
Height: 1.83m (6ft)
Weight: 87.5kg (193lb)
Caps: 25
Points: 322 (4t, 37c, 71p, 5dg)

Morné Steyn made his Springbok debut against the British & Irish Lions in June 2009, then became a national hero when he nailed a last-minute penalty to win the second test (28–25) and the series. He shone in the 2009 Tri-Nations, breaking records by scoring all the Springboks' points in the 31–19 win over New Zealand, setting records for: most points scored by a team's sole scorer; most points in a Tri-Nations game; and most points by a South Africa player against the All Blacks. A week later, he scored 24 points in South Africa's 29–17 win over Australia. By 2010, he was established as South Africa's No. 10 and the deadliest goal-kicker in world Rugby.

Jake White replaced him and the Springboks' fortunes, initially at least, started to change. South Africa won the Tri-Nations in 2004, but then dipped in form ahead of Rugby World Cup 2007. By the time the Springboks arrived in France, however, they were an exciting mix of old and new. They began with a 59–7 victory over Samoa, flattened England (36–0) and romped to the top of the pool with wins over Tonga (30–25) and the United States (64–15). Fiji proved no match in the quarter-finals (37–20), Argentina were demolished in the semi-finals (37–13) and by the time the Springboks faced England in the final they were strong favourites. They won 15–6 to win the Tournament for a second time.

Peter de Villiers took over as coach from White in 2008 – the first non-white South African to take the job – and the Springboks' results since have been mixed: in 2009, they recorded a 2–1 series victory over the British & Irish Lions and won the Tri-Nations for the first time in five years; the following year, however, they managed just one Tri-Nations win in six games. Word from the Springboks is that they are playing the right brand of Rugby to launch a successful title defence and they could just pull off being the first team in history to retain the Rugby World Cup.

They never looked like reclaiming it four years later. Defeat to England (25–6) led to a quarter-final with New Zealand. The All Blacks were too strong, winning 29–9 to send South Africa to their earliest ever Tournament exit. Their team's poor performances may have prompted disappointment among the Rugby-loving public, but that turned to outcry when details of the pre-Tournament preparations emerged. The squad had been sent to Kamp Staaldraad ('Camp Steel Wire') and had, among other things, been forced to sit naked, singing the South Africa national anthem while ice-cold water was poured over them and England's national anthem and New Zealand's *haka* were played at full volume. Soon after, coach Rudolf Straeuli tendered his resignation.

World Champions in 2007, the Springboks will have to fight to defend their crown.

PLAYERS TO WATCH

1. **FOURIE DU PREEZ** Age: 28; Position: scrum-half; Club: Blue Bulls (SA); Caps: 55; Points: 65 (13t)
2. **BRYAN HABANA** Age: 27; Position: wing; Club: Western Province (SA); Caps: 68; Points: 190 (38t)
3. **VICTOR MATFIELD** Age: 33; Position: lock; Club: Blue Bulls (SA); Caps: 105; Points: 35 (7t)
4. **JOHN SMIT** Age: 32; Position: front row/captain; Club: Sharks (SA); Caps: 102; Points: 30 (6t)
5. **PIERRE SPIES** Age: 25; Position: No. 8; Club: Blue Bulls (SA); Caps: 40; Points: 35 (7t)

Wales

Welsh Rugby fans must dream that there had been a Rugby World Cup in the 1970s, when their beloved team was at the peak of its powers. Since then, only a 1987 semi-final berth has provided Welsh fans with something to truly sing about.

The Dragons
www.wru.co.uk

PLAYING STRIP Red shirts with white trim, white shorts, red socks

FORM SINCE RUGBY WORLD CUP 2007

Played: 35
Won: 16
Lost: 18
Drawn: 1
Winning percentage:.......................... 47.14
Points for: 776
Points against:.................................... 789
Points scored per match: 22.17
Points conceded per match: 22.54
Biggest victory: .... 47–8 v Italy
.... at Cardiff on 23 February 2008
Heaviest defeat: .... 42–9 v New Zealand
.... at Dunedin on 19 June 2010

RUGBY WORLD CUP PERFORMANCES

1987	Semi-finals
1991	Group stages
1995	Group stages
1999	Quarter-finals
2003	Quarter-finals
2007	Group stages

One of the ironies of Wales' Rugby World Cup adventures is that their best performance, in 1987, came at a time when expectations were lowest. Wales had endured a miserable run in the Five Nations Championship that year, winning only one of four games and finishing second from bottom. They raised a few eyebrows with a crucial win over Ireland (13–6) in their opening game and subsequent victories over Tonga (29–16) and Canada (40–9) saw them top the pool to earn a quarter-final against a misfiring England side, which they won (16–3). The journey may have come to an abrupt end with a 49–6 defeat to New Zealand in the semi-finals, but try telling that to any Welsh fan: the official version of the story runs that Wales recorded a sensational 22–21 victory over Australia in the third-place match and that Wales were the third-best team in the world. It was one of the worst things that could have happened to Welsh Rugby: victory over an Australia side with little appetite for a bronze medal should not have masked the devastating nature of the defeat to New Zealand. A campaign that should have brought reflection and changes, instead brought misplaced comfort.

The shortcomings in Wales' game were brutally exposed at the 1991 Tournament. They were easily beaten in their opening-game by Samoa (16–13) and were summarily dismissed from the Tournament after losing 38–3 to Australia.

Wales' performance at Rugby World Cup 1995 did little to lift the gloom. As a result of their dire performance four years earlier, they had to qualify, and although they made it through, received a lowly ranking at the pre-Tournament draw,

COACH

WARREN GATLAND

After a successful eight-year playing career with Waikato, Warren Gatland went to the northern hemisphere to make his name as a coach, first with Irish club Galwegians, then with Connacht and finally as coach of the Ireland national team, a position he held for three years before he was sacked in 2001. He rebuilt his reputation with London Wasps and Waikato and was appointed as Wales coach in November 2007. He led Wales to a Grand Slam in 2008 and after a disappointing 2010 Gatland's Wales will be looking to bounce back ahead of Rugby World Cup 2011.

PLAYERS TO WATCH

1. **JAMES HOOK** Age: 25; Position: centre; Club: Ospreys (Wal); Caps: 47; Points: 237 (11t, 34c, 35p, 3dg)
2. **STEPHEN JONES** Age: 33; Position: fly-half; Club: Scarlets (Wal); Caps: 95; Points: 859 (7t, 136c, 178p, 6dg)
3. **MATTHEW REES** Age: 30; Position: hooker/captain; Club: Scarlets (Wal); Caps: 42; Points: 10 (2t)
4. **JAMIE ROBERTS** Age: 24; Position: centre; Club: Cardiff Blues (Wal); Caps: 24; Points: 10 (2t)
5. **ALUN WYN JONES** Age: 25; Position: lock; Club: Ospreys (Wal); Caps: 43; Points: 25 (5t)

England full of confidence. For the first hour of the match it seemed as though a major upset was on the cards, before England rallied to record a 28–17 victory. Wales' performances had provided a real platform to build from.

And they did. In 2005, Wales won their first Grand Slam (in the now-expanded Six Nations) for 27 years. But it was another false dawn: they won only two matches in the competition over the next two years and travelled to Rugby World Cup 2007 woefully out of form. They started well with a win over Canada (42–17), lost to Australia (32–20) and cruised to victory against Japan (72–18) to set up a crucial showdown with Fiji (a team they had beaten six times in six attempts). They crashed to a 38–34 defeat and were dumped out of the Tournament.

Wales' poor performance in the Tournament ultimately cost coach Gareth Jenkins his job. In came Warren Gatland, and Wales responded to his injection of fresh ideas. In 2008, they recorded their second Six Nations Grand Slam in four years, but then slipped back to fourth in 2009 and 2010, yet young blood has inspired Wales of late and they have proven that they are able to play breathtaking attacking Rugby.

If their minimum expectation is to reach the quarter-finals, Wales will have to achieve what they failed to do last time round: they will have to beat Fiji in the group stages.

finding themselves in a tough group alongside Japan, New Zealand and Ireland. After beating Japan (57–10), they lost 34–9 to New Zealand despite a creditable performance. Defeat meant that their final pool match against Ireland became a quarter-final playoff: Ireland scored three tries to two, winning (24–23). Wales suffered their second early Tournament exit in a row.

Just two wins in the 1996 and 1997 Five Nations forced a change – Wales had to improve. In the 1998 Five Nations, they recorded two victories in the Tournament for the first time in four years, then in came Kiwi coach Graham Henry. The team achieved the same the following year and entered Rugby World Cup 1999, for which they were hosts, in high spirits. They beat Argentina (23–18) and Japan (64–15) and, although they lost their final pool match to Samoa (38–31), had done enough to qualify for the quarter-finals for the first time since 1987. They may have lost 24–9 to Australia, but the Tournament had been a respectable outing.

Wales performed with great credit at Rugby World Cup 2003, too. They reeled off three straight victories in their opening games, against Canada (41–10), Tonga (27–20) and Italy (27–15) and although they lost to New Zealand in their final pool match (53–37), had given the All Blacks an almighty scare. They went into their quarter-final match against pre-Tournament favourites

Wales will be looking to avoid their Rugby World Cup 2007 disappointment.

Fiji

Fiji capture the passion and the soul for the Game more than any other nation in world Rugby. This has served them well on the Sevens circuit but hasn't yet translated into major success in the full-scale version of the Game.

The Flying Fijians
www.fijirugby.com

PLAYING STRIP White shirts with black and blue trim, black shorts, black socks

FORM SINCE RUGBY WORLD CUP 2007

Played:	16
Won:	8
Lost:	7
Drawn:	1
Winning percentage:	53.13
Points for:	333
Points against:	413
Points scored per match:	20.81
Points conceded per match:	25.81
Biggest victory:	34–17 v Samoa
	at Lautoka on 7 June 2008
Heaviest defeat:	49–3 v Australia
	at Canberra on 5 June 2010

RUGBY WORLD CUP PERFORMANCES

1987	Quarter-finals
1991	Group stages
1995	Did not qualify
1999	Quarter-final playoffs
2003	Group stages
2007	Quarter-finals

The attractive style in which Fiji play caught the eye from the team's earliest days in international Rugby. In 1939, they caused a stir not only by becoming the first team in history to tour New Zealand unbeaten (seven wins and one draw), but also for the way in which they approached the Game. After watching them play the New Zealand Maoris at Hamilton, the Waikato Times correspondent was moved to describe Fiji's performance as 'the most brilliant exhibition of football seen in Hamilton for many years... Fiji is destined to play a big part in world Rugby'.

That has been the case in Sevens Rugby for decades, but Fiji have always struggled to deal with the extended game and, the occasional shock aside, success has largely eluded them. Their fans point to the fact that, because the majority of their players ply their trade with European clubs, fixtures for the national team – and opportunities for its players to train together – are limited, or that they have lost several eligible players to either New Zealand (Joe Rokocoko and Sitiveni Sivivatu) or Australia (Lote Tuqiri). Both are true, but given the considerable resources at their disposal – 60,000 registered players (more than Ireland, New Zealand or Wales) – Fiji should do better.

COACH

SAM DOMONI

A former player who won six caps for Fiji as a giant lock forward – he stands at 2.06m (6ft 9in) – between 1990 and 1991 and who went on to enjoy a colourful 20-year club career in Australia (with NSW Waratahs and Australia A), England (London Irish and Saracens) and New Zealand (Arataki and Bay of Plenty), Sam Domoni cut his coaching teeth in Australia with Penrith, the Zion Lions and Manly. However, he was still seen as a surprise choice as Fiji's new head coach when he replaced former incumbent Ilivasi Tabua, who was sacked in August 2009.

PLAYERS TO WATCH

1. **SEREMAIA BAI** Age: 32; Position: fly-half; Club: Clermont Auvergne (Fra); Caps: 36; Points: 182 (4t, 27c, 35p, 1dg)
2. **NORMAN LIGAIRI** Age: 35; Position: wing/full-back; Club: La Rochelle (Fra); Caps: 47; Points: 80 (16t)
3. **GABIRIELE LOVOBALAVU** Age: 25; Position: centre; Club: Toulon (Fra); Caps: 11; Points: 5 (1t)
4. **DEACON MANU** Age: 31; Position: prop/captain; Club: Scarlets (Wal); Caps: 5; Points: 0
5. **NAPOLIONI NALAGA** Age: 24; Position: wing; Club: Clermont Auvergne (Fra); Caps: 3; Points: 0

Fiji's first genuine chance to shine on the international stage came at Rugby World Cup 1987. They got off to a dream start, beating Argentina 28–9. It was a crucial win: although they went on to lose their next two matches, against New Zealand (74–13) and Italy (18–15), their opening victory over the Pumas, coupled with the South Americans' subsequent win over the Azzurri, meant that Fiji qualified for the quarter-finals on points difference. They may have lost to France (31–16), but a last-eight appearance, albeit with only one victory, represented a good showing for Fiji.

Which is more than can be said for their performance at Rugby World Cup 1991. In what turned out to be a

STAR PLAYER

SERU RABENI

Position: .... Centre
Born: ....27 December 1978, Bua, Fiji
Club: ....Stade Rochelais (Fra)
Height: 1.88m (6ft 2in)
Weight: 105.7kg (233lb)
Caps: 29
Points: 10 (2t)

Seru Rabeni represented Fiji at U21 and U23 level before winning his first international cap as a replacement against Japan on 20 May 2000. The following year, he took up a three-year course at the University of Otago, allowing him to hone his game on New Zealand's tough domestic Rugby circuit. He played in all four of Fiji's matches at Rugby World Cup 2003 and in all five matches at the 2007 Tournament, during which he emphatically lived up to his reputation as being one of the hardest tacklers in world Rugby. In 2010, after five successful years in England (with Leicester Tigers and Leeds) he moved to French side Stade Rochelais.

miserable Tournament, they slumped to three straight defeats – against Canada (13–3), France (33–9) and Romania (17–15) – and departed the competition early and embarrassed. Worse still was to follow: their poor showing meant that they had to qualify for Rugby World Cup 1995 in South Africa and, in June 1993, they lost a two-legged qualifier against Tonga, 34–26 on aggregate. These were dark days indeed for Fiji's Rugby history.

Their non-qualification gave them a chance to rebuild. The Fiji Rugby Union, hoping to transform a talented bunch of players into a well-drilled unit who could combine a solid execution of the basics with their natural attacking flair, appointed Kiwi Brad Johnstone as coach. The change did the trick: aided by an expanded qualifying Tournament that left Fiji needing just one win against Tonga or the Cook Islands to secure a place at Rugby World Cup 1991, they won both to put the nightmare of their last qualification campaign behind them. In the Tournament itself, they opened with

fine victories over Namibia (67–18) and Canada (38–22) and might have gone on to a hat-trick of wins to top their pool if more calls had gone their way in the Game against France. As it was, they lost the match 28–19 and were forced to play a quarter-final playoff against England, which they lost (45–24).

It was a case of almost but not quite in 2003 as well. Fiji recovered from an

opening-game loss to France (61–18) to edge out the United States (19–18) and Japan (41–13) and set up a final-match against Scotland with the group runners-up spot and a quarter-final place up for grabs. Fiji outscored Scotland by two tries to one, but ill-discipline cost them and the Scots secured a 22–20 victory.

They entered Rugby World Cup 2007 under a new coach, Ilivasi Tabua, who was committed to playing fast, attacking Rugby. They won their opening matches against Japan (35–31) and Canada (29–16), lost heavily to Australia (55–12) and found themselves in a familiar position: needing to win their final pool match against Wales to reach the quarter-finals. In what was the most thrilling match of the Tournament, Graham Dewes crashed over the line in the 76th minute to secure a famous 38–34 Fijian victory. Defeat against South Africa in the last eight mattered little. Fiji were back in Rugby's big time.

The challenges facing Fijian Rugby going into Rugby World Cup 2011 will be made easier by an expanded Test calendar and an emphasis on home-grown talent developed through IRB funded High Performance Centres. The draw has placed them alongside Wales for the second successive Tournament and if Fiji want to achieve their aim of reaching back-to-back quarter-finals for the first time they will need a repeat performance of that memorable 2007 victory. Don't put it past them.

The Fijians will be hoping to repeat the fantastic quarter-final place they earned in 2007.

Samoa

Although one of the most fertile breeding grounds of talent in world Rugby, Samoa's problem has been consistency. But the tough-tackling Samoans have now emerged as a real force in the Game and a much-respected opponent.

Manu Samoa
www.samoarugbyunion.ws

PLAYING STRIP Blue shirts with white trim, white shorts, blue socks

FORM SINCE RUGBY WORLD CUP 2007

Played:	19
Won:	9
Lost:	10
Drawn:	0
Winning percentage:	47.36
Points for:	505
Points against:	469
Points scored per match:	26.58
Points conceded per match:	24.68
Biggest victory:	115–7 v Papua New Guinea at Apia on 11 July 2009
Heaviest defeat:	101–14 v New Zealand at New Plymouth on 3 September 2008

RUGBY WORLD CUP PERFORMANCES

1987	Did not enter
1991	Quarter-finals
1995	Quarter-finals
1999	Quarter-final playoffs
2003	Group stages
2007	Group stages

Rugby is the undisputed number one sport in Samoa: the country has 23,300 registered players from a population of 180,000 and the sport is the true lifeblood of the islands. Rugby came to this remote but beautiful part of the Pacific – situated roughly halfway between Hawaii and New Zealand – with the Marist Brothers in the 1920s and was quick to take hold. The Western Samoan Rugby Football Union was founded in 1924, the same year the country contested its first international match, against Fiji in Apia. Famously, the Game, which Fiji won 6–0, was played at 7am in the morning (so that Samoa's players could go to work) on a pitch with a tree growing in the middle of it.

Despite the country's obvious passion for the Game, however, international fixtures were few and far between, and it wasn't until the start of the annual Pacific Tri-Nations competition in 1982 (a Tournament including Pacific Island neighbours Fiji and Tonga, which Samoa won in the first year) that Samoa started to test their mettle against international opponents on a more regular basis.

Despite not making the cut for the inaugural Rugby World Cup in 1987, Samoa were determined to impress when they finally got their chance to appear on the Game's greatest stage in 1991. Their preparation for the event – for which they comfortably qualified with wins over Korea (74–7), Tonga (12–3) and Japan (37–11) – was thorough in the extreme. In the years before the Tournament, Samoa's Rugby chiefs instigated a recruitment policy to scour New Zealand's Samoan communities for the 'next big thing' before they were spotted by the All Blacks' selectors. It was a policy that would lead to problems for Samoa but, initially at least, it worked.

Samoa's first-ever match in a Rugby World Cup was one for the memory banks: on 6 October 1991, they played Wales at Cardiff Arms Park and out-muscled, outplayed and outscored the home side to reduce the partisan crowd to a stunned silence. Looking at the scoreboard – Western Samoa 16, Wales 13 – one punter famously quipped: 'Thank heavens Wales weren't playing the whole of Samoa.' It was a dark day for the Welsh, but a moment to savour for Samoa. Nor was it a one-off: Samoa gave Australia a real scare before losing 9–3, then recorded a comfortable win over Argentina (35–12) in their final pool match. The journey ended in the quarter-finals with a 28–6 defeat to a strong Scotland side at Murrayfield – but this had been a successful Tournament for Samoa.

COACH

TITIMAEA 'DICKY' TAFUA

A former international prop forward who won 18 caps for Samoa between 1981 and 1989 (captaining them twice), Titimaea 'Dicky' Tafua rose to prominence as a coach with Samoa's Sevens team, leading them to success in both Wellington and Hong Kong in 2007. He replaced Niko Palamo as Samoa's 15-a-side national coach in February 2009. Tragically, he lost his home and several relatives when a tsunami struck the islands of Samoa on 30 September 2009.

STAR PLAYER

MAHONRI SCHWALGER

Position: .... Hooker/captain
Born: .... 15 September 1978, Apia, Samoa
Club: .... Taranaki (NZ)
Height: 1.8m (5ft 11in)
Weight: 106.6kg (235lb)
Caps: 34
Points: 20 (4t)

Born in Samoa but raised in New Zealand (where he played his domestic Rugby with Hawke's Bay and Wellington), Schwalger made his debut for Samoa as a replacement during their 50–6 defeat to Wales in 2000. After six more appearances as a sub over the next four years, he finally made Samoa's starting line-up in the islanders' 18–11 defeat to Scotland in 2005. By 2006 he had made the Samoa No. 2 shirt his own. He appeared in all four of Samoa's matches at Rugby World Cup 2007 and captained his country for the first time against France in 2009, helping Samoa to victory in the Pacific Nations Cup for the first time in 2010.

They performed with distinction at Rugby World Cup 1995 too, reaching the quarter-finals for the second time thanks to wins over Italy (42–18) and Argentina (32–26), before becoming unstuck against a Chester Williams-inspired South Africa and losing 42–14. However, any thoughts of onwards and upwards for Samoan Rugby were shattered with the advent of professionalism. With larger club contracts now on offer, a scouting system that left fewer overseas players spotted by Samoa, and eligibility rules that allowed players to switch allegiance (Va'aiga Tuigamala, Michael Jones and Frank Bunce all played for Samoa before representing the All Blacks), Samoa Rugby started to suffer. As the lure of the New Zealand dollar and dreams of pulling on an All Black shirt grew stronger for kids of Samoan descent growing up in Auckland, so the fortunes of their forefathers' national Rugby team began a gradual decline.

They started Rugby World Cup 1999 with a convincing win over Japan (43–9), but then lost disappointingly to Argentina (32–16) – a team they had beaten in the previous two Tournaments. It meant they had to beat Wales in their final pool match: they emulated the class of 1991 and won 38–31. Victory set up a quarter-final playoff against Scotland, which the Scots won 35–20. It was the first time Samoa had failed to reach the quarter-finals. In 2003, they found themselves in a tough group and, despite comfortably beating Uruguay (60–13) and Georgia (46–9), lost to England (35–22) and South Africa (60–10) to crash out of the Tournament. They fared even worse in 2007, a pool-match victory over the United States (25–21) doing little to lift the gloom of their three opening losses – to South Africa (59–7), Tonga (19–15) and England (44–22).

Samoa have again been placed in the same group as South Africa for the third Tournament in a row, but they can travel to New Zealand for Rugby World Cup 2011 with high hopes, as victories over their other Pool D opponents – Wales, Fiji and Namibia – are more than within their grasp. This will be a defining Tournament for Samoa Rugby.

PLAYERS TO WATCH

1. **FILIPO LEVI** Age: 31; Position: lock; Club: Newcastle Falcons (Eng); Caps: 20; Points: 0
2. **MIKAELE PESAMINO** Age: 27; Position: wing; Club: Vailele (Sam); Caps: 6; Points: 35 (7t)
3. **GEORGE STOWERS** Age: 31; Position: back row; Club: London Irish (Eng); Caps: 17; Points: 15 (3t)
4. **ALESANA TUILAGI** Age: 29; Position: wing; Club: Leicester Tigers (Eng); Caps: 20; Points: 45 (9t)
5. **GAVIN WILLIAMS** Age: 31; Position: centre; Club: Clermont Auvergne (Fra); Caps: 16; Points: 106 (5t, 18c, 15p)

The Samoan rugby team has always earned respect, but in 2011 it will want wins.

Namibia

Namibia have now qualified for four successive Rugby World Cups but the Welwitschias have endured disappointment on Rugby's biggest stage, a trend they will be keen to reverse.

The First World War brought Rugby to Namibia. In 1915, South African troops (as part of a Commonwealth force) invaded the German colony of South-West Africa, and the League of Nations annexed the region to South Africa in 1920. Rugby proved one of the new rulers' more popular pastimes and the locals, particularly the Afrikaners, soon took up the Game. A regional side (retaining the name South-West Africa) competed annually in South Africa's Currie Cup, without a great deal of success – apart from 1989, when they finished third – and also hosted matches against the British Lions (in 1962, 1968, 1974 and 1980). In short, the region was an established but isolated backwater of South African Rugby. In 1990, however, it was time for change: a 20-year civil war ended with independence from South Africa, and Namibia was born.

The country took no time to leap into the international Rugby fold: the Namibia Rugby Union was formed in March 1990; the country joined the IRB in the same year; and their fledgling international career got off to a spectacular start. In 1991, their first full year, they recorded back-to-back wins over an up-and-coming Italy side (17–7 and 33–19), an even more impressive pair of wins over Ireland (15–6 and 26–15) and ended the year with a record of played ten won ten. Their performances surprised everyone: the Welwitschias may well have been match-hardened after years of plying their trade on South Africa's domestic circuit, but no one had expected them to achieve such instant success. Greater tests, however, were still to come.

Namibia's IRB membership had come too late for Rugby World Cup 1991, so the first opportunity to take what had been an electrifying start to international Rugby and turn it into a statement of future intent came in the qualifiers for RWC 1995 Tournament, due to be staged in South Africa of all places. The incentives for Namibia to be a part of Rugby's biggest festival were huge.

They started their campaign with comfortable victories over the Arabian Gulf (64–20), Kenya (60–9) and Zimbabwe (41–26) to progress to a four-team round-robin Tournament in Casablanca (alongside Morocco, the Ivory Coast and Zimbabwe) with one berth in the Tournament and one place in the final repechage round up for grabs. Namibia opened with a 25–20 victory over Zimbabwe and then, confident of victory in their second match against the Ivory Coast, opted to make eight changes to rest players for what would be the crunch encounter against Morocco. They paid a high price, losing 13–12 to the Ivory Coast and drawing 16–16 with Morocco to exit the Tournament. Not only was it a bitter pill to swallow, it came in the closing stages of the international careers of many of the players who had helped Namibia to settle

COACH

JOHAN DIERGAARDT

Formerly the head coach of Namibia-based club Western Suburbs and the chairman of the Welwitschias' national selection committee, Johan Diergaardt served as assistant coach to John Williams before being appointed as national coach following Williams' resignation in November 2009 to take up a coaching position in South Africa. His tenure got off to a disappointing start when Namibia suffered a home defeat to Russia (30–15) in January 2010, but later in the year he made the headlines when he led the Welwitschias to victories over Romania (21–17), Scotland A (23–20) and Georgia (21–16) to win the IRB Nations Cup.

Welwitschias
www.namibianrugby.com

PLAYING STRIP Blue shirt with white, red and yellow trim, blue shorts, black socks

FORM SINCE RUGBY WORLD CUP 2007
Played:	12
Won:	8
Lost:	3
Drawn:	1
Winning percentage:	70.83
Points for:	256
Points against:	210
Points scored per match:	21.33
Points conceded per match:	17.50
Biggest victory:	54–14 v Ivory Coast
	at Windhoek on 27 June 2009
Heaviest defeat:	30–15 v Russia
	at Windhoek on 23 January 2010

RUGBY WORLD CUP PERFORMANCES
1987	Did not enter
1991	Did not enter
1995	Did not qualify
1999	Group stages
2003	Group stages
2007	Group stages

STAR PLAYER

JACQUES BURGER

Position: ....Back row/captain
Born: .... 29 July 1983, Windhoek, Namibia
Club: ....Saracens (Eng)
Height: 1.88m (6ft 2in)
Weight: 106kg (234lb)
Caps: 25
Points: 20 (4t)

Burger made his international debut against Zambia in August 2004 and played his early domestic Rugby for South African Currie Cup side Griquas. He first made his name at Rugby World Cup 2007 in France, putting in some standout performances in a losing cause, particularly during Namibia's 32–17 defeat to Ireland, to earn a contract with Super 14 outfit the Bulls, but it was a move to Guinness Premiership outfit Saracens in the 2009–10 season that ignited his career: quick, ruthless and fearless on the floor and equally destructive with ball in hand, this outstanding back-row forward helped Namibia to victory in the IRB Nations Cup in December 2010.

They qualified for Rugby World Cup 2003, too – thanks to a nerve-jangling 43–42 aggregate win over Tunisia – but once again found the Tournament to be a chastening experience. They lost all four matches – against Argentina (67–14), Ireland (64–7), Australia (142–0 – the heaviest defeat in the competition's history) and Romania (37–7), scored a paltry 28 points and conceded a mighty 310 (an all-time Rugby World Cup record).

It was more of the same in 2007: after suffering early qualifying defeats to Tunisia (24–7) and Kenya (30–26), they secured a place in the Tournament with a 52–15 victory over Morocco. Yet again, however, they failed to cope with the step-up in class and lost all of their matches for the third consecutive time – against Ireland (32–17), France (87–10), Argentina (63–3) and Georgia (30–0). It may not have been as bad as 2003, but the bare statistics damned Namibia: they had played 11 matches in the Tournament and lost every one of them.

They secured a place at their fourth consecutive Rugby World Cup with an unbeaten qualifying campaign, but the draw for the 2011 Tournament has not been kind and they find themselves in a tough group (perhaps their toughest yet) alongside South Africa, Wales, Fiji and Samoa. It's hard to see the Welwitschias Tournament record changing.

so comfortably into international Rugby. It was a huge opportunity missed and one from which Namibian Rugby has failed to recover – five more years of third-tier African Rugby did little to inspire a new generation of players.

They made amends at Rugby World Cup 1999 qualifiers, though, recovering from a shock opening defeat to Tunisia (20–17) to record victories over Zimbabwe twice (32–26 and 39–14), the Ivory Coast (22–10) and Morocco (17–8) to secure a place at the Tournament finals for the first time. When the Tournament finally got underway Namibia lost all three matches – against Fiji (67–18), France (47–13) and Canada (72–11) – and departed having conceded more points than any other team bar Italy (186 points to the Azzurri's 196).

Namibia celebrate their surprise victory at the 2010 IRB Nations Cup.

WILKINSON'S WONDER STRIKE
22 NOVEMBER 2003, TELSTRA STADIUM, SYDNEY

It was a dramatic conclusion to a pulsating final. England, the world's No. 1 ranked team, and hosts Australia were locked at 17–17 in Rugby World Cup 2003 final with only one-and-a-half minutes of the second period of extra-time remaining. England won a lineout 6m (20ft) from Australia's 22; Lewis Moody won the ball for England; Mike Catt took the crash ball into Australia's defence; scrum-half Matt Dawson scythed through a gap and stormed into Australia's 22; and, after what seemed like an age, the ball, with 31 seconds remaining on the clock, found its way back to Jonny Wilkinson, sitting deep in the pocket with only one thought on his mind – drop-goal. He nailed the attempt with his right boot and, to the delight of England fans, the ball sailed through the uprights. England crept into a 20–17 lead and hung on to secure a famous victory.

Jonny Wilkinson's right boot won England a dramatic Rugby World Cup victory in 2003.

The Stars

There is no finer stage upon which to attain a legendary status within the Game than at Rugby World Cup and plenty of players have done just that over the years. In 1987, Michael Jones and Grant Fox shone for New Zealand, and who could forget Serge Blanco's last-gasp, semi-final try? In 1991, a pair of Wallabies – Michael Lynagh and David Campese – stole the limelight, while New Zealand's Jonah Lomu simply stole the next two shows. Jonny Wilkinson's golden boot shone for England in 2003, while in France four years later, Bryan Habana blazed a scorching trail for South Africa. The following section takes a closer look at the prime candidates at Rugby World Cup 2011 to join the pantheon of all-time Tournament greats.

The All Blacks' Dan Carter (centre) celebrates with Kieran Read (left) after scoring a try against Wales in June 2010.

Dan Carter New Zealand

Blessed with a devastating burst of speed, a line-breaking side-step and a robust defence, as well as being a goal-kicker of metronomic accuracy and a master tactician, Dan Carter is vying to be the leading points-scorer in international history and the most accomplished fly-half in world Rugby.

Dan Carter made his Super Rugby debut for the Crusaders in 2003 and became a senior All Black later the same year, making his debut at inside-centre, at the age of 21, against Wales at Hamilton on 21 June and scoring 20 points (one try, six conversions and a penalty) in New Zealand's comprehensive 55–3 victory. He earned a place in the All Blacks' Rugby World Cup 2003 squad, but played in only three matches and watched on from the bench as New Zealand crashed out of the Tournament to hosts Australia in the semi-finals.

A string of strong performances in 2004 saw him wrestle the New Zealand No. 10 jersey from Carlos Spencer and in 2005 he was the star of the series against the British & Irish Lions. He scored 11 points in New Zealand's 21–3 victory in the first test, but it was his performance in the second test in Wellington that catapulted his reputation to new heights. Producing one of the finest displays by a fly-half in recent memory, Carter scored two tries, four conversions and five penalties (a haul of 33 points) to help New Zealand to a series-clinching 48–18 victory. Injury may have ruled him out of the third and final test, but Carter's star had never shone brighter. He ended the year as the IRB Player of the Year.

The good form continued into 2006, with 25 points during the All Blacks' 35–17 victory over South Africa the highlight of a successful Tri-Nations campaign, but if the following year was the moment when the world's most dazzling player was supposed to lift the

game's most glittering prize, the script turned sour. New Zealand, off the back of a third successive Tri-Nations title, travelled to Rugby World Cup 2007 as overwhelming favourites only to be dumped out of the Tournament by France in the quarter-finals.

New Zealand roared back in 2008, winning a fourth consecutive Tri-Nations crown, before Carter took up a £30,000-a-game contract with Perpignan in France. He played only five games before a recurring Achilles injury brought his Mediterranean adventure to a premature halt. After re-signing for Crusaders, he was back in black in 2009 and made a majestic return to international Rugby by kicking a last-gasp penalty in New Zealand's 19–18 victory over Australia in Sydney – one of the few highlights in what had been an otherwise disappointing campaign for the All Blacks.

With Carter back at the fly-half helm there would be no such disappointment in 2010. New Zealand cruised to the Tri-Nations title and finished the year with a Grand Slam-winning tour to Europe, during which Carter overtook England's Jonny Wilkinson as the leading points-scorer in international Rugby history.

FACTS AND FIGURES

Born: ....5 March 1982,
................................Leeston, New Zealand
Position: ....Fly-half
Club: ....Crusaders (NZ)
Height: 1.78m (5ft 10in)
Weight: 92.1kg (203lb)
Caps: 79
Debut: ....v Wales at Hamilton
....................................on 21 June 2003
Points: 1,188 (29t, 208c, 207p, 2dg)

The linchpin of New Zealand's back division, Dan Carter is central to the All Blacks' hopes.

Tom Croft England

An explosive runner, making him a dangerous opponent in attack either with the ball in hand or as a support runner, and a supremely effective lineout jumper, England flanker Tom Croft is one of the most exciting prospects to have burst on to the international Rugby scene in recent years.

FACTS AND FIGURES

Born: ....7 November 1985,
.... Basingstoke, England
Position: ....Flanker
Club: .... Leicester Tigers (Eng)
Height: 1.96m (6ft 5in)
Weight: 104.8kg (231lb)
Caps: 22
Debut: ....v France at Stade de France,
........................Paris, on 23 February 2008
Points: 5 (1t)

Described by former All Black Aaron Mauger as the fastest forward he had ever seen in world Rugby and by former England No. 8 Dean Richards as a player who has 'everything', Tom Croft made his senior debut for the Leicester Tigers in the 2005–06 season (against Gloucester a week after his 20th birthday) and the following year made 16 appearances during the Tigers' charge to the title, was a key member of the England U21 side that won a Six Nations Championship Grand Slam and played for the England Saxons team at the Churchill Cup (scoring the decisive try – a blistering 60m (65yd) dash – to beat the New Zealand Maoris in the final). The 2007–08 season, however, is considered to have been his breakthrough year. He produced a Man of the Match-winning performance against Cardiff in the Heineken Cup semi-final (although Leicester went on to lose in the Final to Leinster, 19–16), claimed a second successive Guinness Premiership winners' medal and won his first cap for England when he came off the bench in their 24–15 Six Nations victory over France in Paris, impressing enough to earn a place in the starting line-up for England's final games of the campaign against Scotland and Ireland.

After the successful 2009 Six Nations campaign – the highlight of which saw him pick up the Man of the Match award for his performance during England's 34–10 victory over France at Twickenham – he earned a late call-up (as a replacement for Ireland's Alan Quinlan) to the British & Irish Lions tour to South Africa. He played in all three tests (scoring a brace of tries in the first in Durban, incredible for a Lions debutant) and, although the Lions campaign may have culminated in a disappointing 2–1 series defeat, ended a stellar year among the nominees for the IRB Player of the Year – becoming the first Englishman to appear on the list since Jonny Wilkinson in 2003.

A knee injury saw him miss out on the 2010 Six Nations Championship, but Croft made an impressive return to action, playing a full 80 minutes in both of his side's back-to-back, home-and-away victories over Australia (21–20 at Sydney and 35–18 at Twickenham). He put in some solid displays – particularly in the lineout – during the remainder of England's 2010 autumn internationals until he fractured his scapula in the final match of the year against South Africa. The injury kept him out of the first three games of the 2011 Six Nations Championship. England will need him fully fit if they are to become the first team in history to reach three successive Rugby World Cup Finals in New Zealand in 2011.

A dynamic back-row forward, Tom Croft has made a blistering start to his international career.

Fourie du Preez South Africa

A star for South Africa during their successful Rugby World Cup 2007 campaign, Fourie du Preez has established a reputation as being one of the smartest performers in world Rugby. He will need to be at his best if the Springboks are to become the first team in history to defend their world title.

Dubbed by New Zealand coach Graham Henry as the best scrum-half in world Rugby, Fourie du Preez is one of that rare breed of player who excels as much when he is not on the ball as when he is on it. He provides an excellent service from the base of the scrum, possesses sublime kicking skills and not only an eye for the gap but also the pace to take him through it, the attributes all the great scrum-halves over the years have had in common. What sets the Pretoria-born No. 9 apart, however, is his innate and sublime ability to read the game, sense the danger, put himself in the line of fire and nullify the situation: it is a quality that has saved many of his teams on numerous occasions over the years.

He made his provincial debut for the Blue Bulls as a teenager in 2002 and was a standout member of the South Africa U21 side (coached by Jake White) that won that year's U21 Rugby World Championship. When White was appointed coach of the national side following Rugby World Cup 2003, it did not take him long to remember du Preez's qualities – or the lack of direction at half-back that had cost the Springboks dear in Rugby World Cup 2003 – and the new coach handed his former charge an international debut in June 2004, against Ireland in Bloemfontein. It was clear from the start that du Preez's association with the Springboks was going to be a lengthy one.

In 2004, he played a part in all four of the Springboks' matches as they won their first Tri-Nations title since 1998,

consolidated his place in the side and ended 2006 voted his country's Player of the Year. It was his performances during Rugby World Cup 2007, however, that set tongues wagging: du Preez pulled the strings in six of the Springboks' seven matches – scoring tries against the United States (in the group matches) and against Argentina (in the semi-finals) – as they marched to their second world title.

If it was more of the same in 2008, then du Preez's already glowing reputation hit new heights during a 2009 season that saw him shine for South Africa as the Boks recorded a 2–1 series win over the British & Irish Lions, won their third Tri-Nations title and ended the year ranked the No. 1 side in world Rugby. Du Preez ended the season among the nominees for the IRB Player of the Year award. He underwent surgery in June 2010 to solve a long-standing shoulder problem, but is expected to have recovered in time for Rugby World Cup 2011.

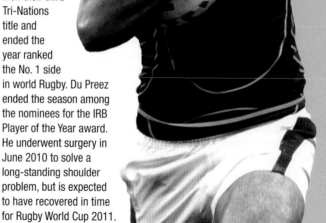

South Africa will need Fourie du Preez to be fit and firing at Rugby World Cup 2011.

Matt Giteau Australia

Still only 28 years of age and fast approaching 100 caps in international Rugby, Matt Giteau is one of the most talented players of his generation, and also one of the most versatile: he has represented Australia in three positions over the years – at inside-centre, fly-half and scrum-half.

FACTS AND FIGURES

Born: .... 29 September 1982,
.... Sydney, Australia
Position: Inside-centre, fly-half, scrum-half
Club: .... ACT Brumbies (Aus)
Height: 1.78m (5ft 10in)
Weight: 84.8kg (187lb)
Caps: 91
Debut: .... v England at Twickenham
.... on 16 November 2002
Points: 666 (28t, 101c, 104p, 4dg)

A former pupil at St Edmund's College in Canberra (the same school that nurtured George Gregan), Matt Giteau played for Australia's Sevens and U21 sides in 2001 and, given that he had yet to make his Super 12 debut, was a surprise selection for the Wallabies tour to the northern hemisphere for the 2002 autumn internationals (during which he won his first cap, from the bench) during Australia's 32–31 defeat to England at Twickenham. He announced his arrival on the international stage in his first start, by scoring a hat-trick of tries against Namibia at Rugby World Cup 2003, and made an appearance in the Final against England as a replacement.

It wasn't until 2004, however, that he became a firmly established member of the Australia line-up, when he started 11 of the Wallabies' 12 tests (at inside-centre) and ended the season among the nominees for the IRB Player of the Year award. He bounced back from a knee injury with a two-try haul and a Man of the Match performance in the Wallabies' record 49–0 win over South Africa in Brisbane in 2006 and made an experimental switch to scrum-half at the end of the year. He switched back to his more customary midfield role for the Tri-Nations and Rugby World Cup 2007 Tournaments and made headlines when he switched from ACT Brumbies to Western Force in a reported A$4.5 million deal (making him the highest paid Rugby player, of either code, in Australia).

The high-profile move made little impact on his form. In 2008, back at fly-half, he achieved an 85 per cent kicking success rate during the course of the season to move up to eighth on Australia's all-time points-scoring list. He showed his continued value to the team in 2009 by contributing all of the Wallabies' points (one try, one conversion and five penalties) during their 22–6 victory over France in Sydney, before going on to score 72 points in that year's Tri-Nations (a single-season record for an Australia player in the competition) and ended the season both as that year's leading international points-scorer (with 153) and among the nominees for the IRB Player of the Year for the second time in his career.

The introduction of Quade Cooper saw him switch back to inside-centre in 2010 and still going strong: he is one of only four players in Tri-Nations history to have accumulated more than 250 points; stands eighth on his country's all-time points-scoring list (with 666), sixth on the Wallabies' all-time appearances list (with 91) and will be appearing at his third Rugby World Cup in New Zealand in 2011. The whole of Australia hopes it will be third time lucky for this talented player.

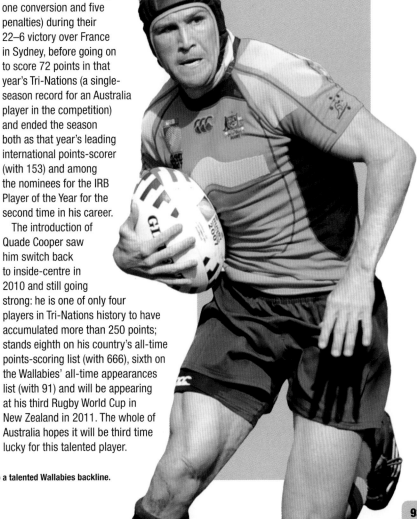

Matt Giteau brings experience and a touch of class to a talented Wallabies backline.

Imanol Harinordoquy France

Hailed as a star prospect when he put in some barnstorming performances for France in his debut season in international Rugby, Imanol Harinoroduy has suffered the slings and arrows of the game's fortune, but was back to his best in 2010. He has a huge role to play for France at Rugby World Cup 2011.

Known simply as 'Imanol' in his native France, Bayonne-born Harinordoquy is a Basque through and through; he is a huge supporter of the region's culture and, when he is not playing Rugby, runs his family's traditional cattle-trading business – a commitment that has seen him sign a series of one-year deals with his clubs over the years to give him greater flexibility. He took up playing Rugby seriously at the age of 14 and excelled, progressing to the France U19 and U21 teams, the latter as captain. He made a sensational debut for France, aged 21, against Wales in the 2002 Six Nations Championship and marked his second cap with a try against England as France went on to claim both the championship and the Grand Slam.

He was part of a formidable French back row – alongside stalwarts Olivier Magne and Serge Betsen – that travelled to Rugby World Cup 2003. The trio shone during Les Bleus' 43–21 quarter-final win over Ireland (with Imanol scoring one of his side's four tries), but were outplayed during their semi-final defeat to England, with the notorious English press singling out Harinordoquy as the focus of their glee, labelling the No. 8 'Harry Ordinary'. It was an undeserving tag for a player who had ended the season among the nominees for the IRB Player of the Year award and Imanol bounced back with some bullying displays in the 2004 Six Nations, finishing the Tournament with tries against Italy (two), Wales and England –

as France romped to the title with Grand Slam-winning swagger.

And then injury struck – a separated shoulder suffered while playing for Biarritz. Harinordoquy's return to form and fitness was a lengthy one: he made only three appearances for Les Bleus in 2005 and 2006, but won a call-up to France's Rugby World Cup 2007 squad and seemed to be back in favour when he was named in the starting line-up for France's opening game against Argentina. However, the Pumas pulled off a shock 17–12 victory and Harinordoquy did not appear in the starting line-up again until the third-place playoff match. Worse was to follow: when new coach Marc Lièvremont took over the reins after the Tournament he jettisoned the Bayonne man from the squad altogether.

Yet again he bounced back, producing some stellar performances for Biarritz in the Heineken Cup to win back his place in the national side and by 2009 he appeared to be back to his best – as evidenced by his spectacular one-handed try against Ireland at Croke Park. Now one of the first names on Lièvremont's teamsheet, expect him to shine at Rugby World Cup 2011.

At his best, Basque No. 8 Imanol Harinordoquy can be a marauding menace for France.

FACTS AND FIGURES

Born:	20 February 1980, Bayonne, France
Position:	No. 8
Club:	Biarritz (Fra)
Height:	1.93m (6ft 4in)
Weight:	104.8kg (231lb)
Caps:	64
Debut:	v Wales at Millennium Stadium on 16 February 2002
Points:	60 (12t)

James Hook Wales

Great distribution, acute awareness of the state of play and an exhilarating running style that evokes Welsh Rugby's glory years all make James Hook one of the brightest young talents in world Rugby. Rugby World Cup 2011 will be the ideal platform for him to fulfil his world-class potential.

James Hook enjoyed great success with Neath RFC – breaking the club record for the most points in a single season – before signing for Ospreys in 2004. His rise through the Ospreys' ranks may not have been instantaneous, but a string of commanding performances at both fly-half and inside-centre from 2005 onwards saw his reputation catapult and he made his international debut for Wales against Argentina in June 2006, scoring a try in a narrow 27–25 defeat. His home debut, when he came on as a replacement against Australia at the Millennium Stadium on 4 November 2006, saw his stock rise even higher: he scored 13 points in the pulsating 29–29 draw and picked up the Man of the Match award.

Hook kept his place in the Wales squad for the 2007 Six Nations, but struggled to make his mark at inside-centre, and it took a switch to fly-half for the final fixture of the campaign, against England at the Millennium Stadium, to bring the best out of him: he put in a Man of the Match-winning display, scoring a full-house haul of 22 points (one try, one conversion, four penalties and a drop-goal) as Wales won 27–18. But that was where the good news ended for both Wales and Hook in 2007: a poor showing at that year's Rugby World Cup (Wales were dumped out of the competition at the group stages) led to a change in coach and the need for Wales' players to restore their damaged reputations.

Hook responded in style in the 2008 Six Nations, contributing 16 points in the 26–19 win over England at Twickenham and a breakaway try against Scotland in Cardiff, as Wales secured their second Grand Slam in four years. No one doubted Hook's class, but as Stephen Jones returned to form at fly-half for Wales, the question loomed as to where to play him. Initially, at least, the answer seemed to be nowhere: Hook made only one start in the 2009 Six Nations campaign, playing in the penultimate match of the season, against Italy.

Although he missed out on selection for the British & Irish Lions tour of South Africa, he was drafted into the squad and, despite missing out on a test cap, produced some stirring performances for the midweek team. By 2010, he had secured a place in the Wales line-up at centre, and his partnership with Jamie Roberts, a star of the 2009 Lions tour, threatens to become one of the most potent in the international game. The world has yet to see the best of James Hook and New Zealand 2011 will be his best chance yet to shine.

James Hook adds a touch of dazzle to Wales' talented back division.

FACTS AND FIGURES

Born: ....27 June 1985,
....Neath, Wales
Position: ... Inside-centre, fly-half, full-back
Club: .... Ospreys (Wal)
Height: 1.83m (6ft)
Weight: 91.6kg (202lb)
Caps: 47
Debut: .... v Argentina at Puerto Madryn
.... on 21 June 2006
Points: 237 (11t, 34c, 35p, 3dg)

Richie McCaw New Zealand

The only three-time winner of the IRB Player of the Year award and a player fast cementing his place among the all-time greats of the game, Richie McCaw's otherwise glittering Rugby career lacks only one honour: Rugby World Cup success. That could all change in 2011.

Richie McCaw played for New Zealand U19 in 1999, for the U21 in 2000 and made his senior debut, aged 20, against Ireland in November 2001. He put in an eye-catching display, showing all the qualities that would make him the standout player of his generation and ended the year by winning the IRB Newcomer of the Year.

He nailed down a permanent place in the All Blacks line-up, playing a leading role in New Zealand's Tri-Nations wins in 2002 and 2003, and was his country's standout player in a disappointing Rugby World Cup 2003 campaign that ended with defeat to hosts Australia in the semi-finals. McCaw captained the All Blacks for the first time, aged 23, against Wales in November 2004 (a 26–25 victory) and, the following year, noticeably sharpened the skills that would propel his career to new heights. The Rugby world sat up to take notice of his great qualities: he is a tireless worker, robust in defence, a master at the breakdown and, with a surprising burst of pace and deft handling skills, a more than useful link in attack. He was appointed captain on a permanent basis in May 2006 and led the All Blacks to Tri-Nations success in his first season at the helm (at the end of which he won the IRB Player of the Year for the first time) and to the defence of their title the following year. The Holy Grail, however, Rugby World Cup 2007, lay ahead.

Not for the first time, New Zealand entered the Tournament as the No. 1 ranked team in the world and as firm favourites to end their 20-year competition drought. McCaw led from the front and scored two tries during a 76–14 victory over Italy as New Zealand eased into the quarter-finals to face a faltering France side that was still licking its wounds after a shock opening-game defeat to Argentina. But the French found fluency where they had previously misfired and won the match 20–18. It represented New Zealand's worst-ever performance in the Tournament and, amid huge disappointment, much of the criticism was levelled at McCaw's leadership.

The captain responded in spectacular fashion: leading the All Blacks to the 2008 Tri-Nations title and to a Grand Slam tour of the northern hemisphere later in the year. In 2009 he became the first player in history to win the IRB Player of the Year for a second time and won it for the third time in 2010 (the same year he led the All Blacks to a fourth Tri-Nations title in five years). One senses that success or failure at Rugby World Cup 2011 will ultimately define his career.

The New Zealand captain is, quite simply, the best player of his generation.

FACTS AND FIGURES

Born: .... 31 December 1980,
.... Oamaru, New Zealand
Position: .... Flanker
Club: .... Crusaders (NZ)
Height: 1.88m (6ft 2in)
Weight: 105.7kg (233lb)
Caps: 94
Debut: ....v Ireland at Lansdowne Road
.... on 17 November 2001
Points: 95 (19t)

Victor Matfield South Africa

A Rugby World Cup winner in 2007, the most capped South Africa player in history and considered by many observers of the game to be the best lock forward in world Rugby, Victor Matfield has been the cornerstone of a powerful South Africa pack for the best part of a decade.

A former South Africa U21 international, Victor Matfield made his senior debut for the Springboks as a replacement against Italy at Port Elizabeth on 30 June 2001. It was his sheer athleticism that marked him out as a special player, making him a supreme lineout jumper and a real threat in the loose. He made his first start for South Africa in the 2001 Tri-Nations and scored his first international try against Italy during the end-of-year tour to Europe.

He started alongside long-time second-row partner Bakkies Botha for the first time against Scotland in 2003 and played in four of South Africa's matches at Rugby World Cup 2003, including the quarter-final defeat to the All Blacks. He was one of the few constants in the side as new coach Jake White chopped and changed the line-up in an attempt to find a winning formula and was a commanding figure during South Africa's successful 2004 Tri-Nations campaign, scoring a try in the title-clinching, final-match 23–19 victory over Australia in Durban. It was South Africa's first win in the competition for six years.

A string of solid performances in 2005 saw Matfield named among the nominees for the IRB Player of the Year award for the first, and surprisingly only, time in his career. He led his country for the first time in 2007 against New Zealand – the first of several stand-in stints as captain – and shone at Rugby World Cup 2007, featuring in all seven of the Springboks' matches and

putting in a Man of the Match-winning performance during their 15–6 victory over England in the Final. He was many people's pick as the player of the Tournament.

In 2008, in the absence of the injured John Smit, Matfield led South Africa to a memorable 30–28 victory over New Zealand in Dunedin to end the All Blacks' five-year unbeaten home record. The following year he played in all three tests against the touring British & Irish Lions and domination of the lineout was a key factor behind the Springboks' 2–1 series success. He carried his form into the 2009 Tri-Nations, which South Africa won for only the third time in their history.

In 2010, he became only the third South Africa player in history to reach the 100-cap milestone (alongside Percy Montgomery and Smit) and passed Montgomery's national record haul of 102 caps against Wales at the Millennium Stadium on 13 November, marking the occasion by scoring his seventh international try. Rugby World Cup 2011 will be Matfield's last chance to shine on the game's biggest stage and the long-serving lock will be determined to bow out in style.

FACTS AND FIGURES

Born: ....11 May 1977,
............................Pietersburg, South Africa
Position: ....Lock
Club: .... Blue Bulls (SA)
Height: 2.01m (6ft 7in)
Weight: 112.5kg (248lb)
Caps: 105
Debut: .... v Italy at Port Elizabeth
....on 30 June 2001
Points: 35 (7t)

Victor Matfield has been the best lineout jumper in world Rugby for the best part of a decade.

Brian O'Driscoll Ireland

The best centre in world Rugby and the finest player in the northern hemisphere over the last decade, Brian O'Driscoll is Ireland's all-time leading try-scorer, his country's longest-serving and most successful captain and still one of the most feared opponents in the international game.

O'Driscoll was a prominent member of the Ireland side that won the U19 Rugby World Championship in France in 1998 and he won his first senior cap, aged 20, on 12 June 1999, against Australia in Brisbane. He went on to play in all four of Ireland's matches at Rugby World Cup 1999, scoring his first international try against the United States, before the men in green crashed out of the Tournament to Argentina in the quarter-final playoffs. But better times lay ahead for the talented centre.

In 2000, he stole the headlines when he scored a hat-trick of tries against France to hand Ireland their first win in Paris for 28 years. The following year he was picked for the British & Irish Lions tour to Australia and appeared in all three tests, scoring a sensational, defence-splitting solo try in the first test victory in Brisbane. The Lions may well have lost the series 2–1, but O'Driscoll's contribution to the cause had been considerable.

He put in another headline-grabbing performance for Ireland during their 2002 Six Nations clash against Scotland at Lansdowne Road, scoring a hat-trick of tries during a 43–22 victory, and captained his country for the first time (in the absence of regular captain Keith Wood) in November later in the year. He made his next Rugby World Cup appearance in 2003, scoring three tries in the Tournament – one against Australia and two in Ireland's 43–21 quarter-final defeat to France.

He took over from Keith Wood as Ireland captain in 2004 and led his side to a Triple Crown-winning second place in the Six Nations and, in 2005, was named as British & Irish Lions captain for their tour to New Zealand – becoming the first Irishman to receive the honour since Ciaran Fitzgerald in 1983. What should have been the highlight of his career turned into a horror show, however, when he suffered a badly dislocated shoulder just minutes into the opening test and missed the rest of the tour.

He bounced back in style in 2006, leading Ireland to their second Six Nations Triple Crown in three years – clinched with a pulsating 28–24 victory over England at Twickenham – and was voted the Player of the Tournament. He shone as Ireland secured another Triple Crown in 2007 (collecting the Player of the Tournament award for the second successive year) and travelled to the Rugby World Cup with high hopes. They were duly dashed when Ireland foundered in the group stages. A disappointing 2008 Six Nations campaign was followed by a memorable one in 2009: O'Driscoll led Ireland to their first Grand Slam in 61 years. In 2010, he became one of only three Irishmen to reach the 100-cap milestone.

Rugby World Cup 2011 will be Brian O'Driscoll's fourth appearance at the Tournament.

FACTS AND FIGURES

Born: ....21 January 1979,
.... Dublin, Ireland
Position: ....Centre
Club: ....Leinster (Ire)
Height: 1.78m (5ft 10in)
Weight: 95.3kg (210lb)
Caps: 107
Debut: ....v Australia at Brisbane
.... on 12 June 1999
Points: 220 (41t, 5dg)

Morgan Parra France

A relative newcomer to international Rugby, Morgan Parra's qualities – great tactical awareness, a surprising turn of pace and innate leadership skills – suggest he will be an integral part of the France team for many years to come and that he could well go on to become one of the game's greats.

FACTS AND FIGURES

Born: .... 15 November 1988,
....Metz, France
Position: ....Scrum-half
Club: ....Clermont Auvergne (Fra)
Height: 1.8m (5ft 11in)
Weight: 76.2kg (168lb)
Caps: 22
Debut: ....v Scotland at Murrayfield
....on 3 February 2008
Points: 134 (0t, 22c, 29p, 1dg)

Morgan Parra was a standout player for France in junior international Rugby, playing for the U18 team and then as captain of the U19 squad that finished fifth at the 2007 U19 Rugby World Championship and also shone on the club circuit for Bourgoin. It was soon clear that this was a player with a precocious talent. He was propelled into the senior squad and made his international debut, aged 19, as a replacement against Scotland at Murrayfield on 3 February 2008 – a match France won 27–6. Never shy to voice an opinion, he rattled a few cages in the build-up to France's next match, against Ireland, with an ill-advised attack on the legality of Ireland's defensive play and started the game from the bench. He was handed a first full start in France's third match of the Six Nations campaign, against England at the Stade de France, and formed a youthful half-back pairing with François Trinh-Duc (who only had two caps to his name). The pair, dubbed the new French generation, struggled and France slipped to a 24–13 defeat and finished third in the championship.

Parra suffered further disappointment at club level: Bourgoin were eliminated from the Heineken Cup at the group stages and finished ninth in France's Top 14 to miss out on European Rugby for the first time in seven years. He ended a frustrating year by captaining France U20 at the IRB Junior World Championship in Wales. Parra unfortunately suffered a hand injury early in the Tournament, and France finished in sixth place.

He recovered to appear in all five of France's 2009 Six Nations matches (three of them from the start) and continued to impress, showing charismatic leadership qualities from the base of the scrum. He carried his form into club Rugby, playing a leading role as Bourgoin marched into the European Challenge Cup Final – only to suffer a dislocated shoulder during the 15–3 defeat to Northampton Saints.

For all the promise of his early years, however, 2009–10 was the season when Parra showed his world-class potential. After signing for Clermont Auvergne in the close season, he started from the bench in France's autumn internationals (having slipped behind Julien Dupuy in the pecking order). But a string of impressive performances at club level propelled him into the starting line-up for France's 2010 Six Nations opener against Scotland (a comfortable 18–9 win) and went on to prove his exceptional talent as he bossed France's forwards and cajoled their backs to a Grand Slam win. Now established as France's first-choice scrum-half, Rugby fans are still to see the very best of Morgan Parra and Rugby World Cup 2011 could well be his chance to shine.

Morgan Parra has the qualities required to become one of the greats of the game.

Alesana Tuilagi Samoa

The latest in the long line of talent to have emerged from Samoa in recent years, Alesana Tuilagi is a giant of a man, standing 1.85m (6ft 1in) tall and weighing a colossal 116.6kg (257lb), but possessing a sprinter's pace and a ballerina's balance. He is one of the most potent finishers in world Rugby.

Born in Apia, the Samoan capital, in 1981, Rugby formed a considerable part of Alesana Tuilagi's youth (four of his brothers went on to play the game professionally) and he was selected to tour with the national team for the first time aged 19, in 2000, but did not win a cap. Shortly afterwards, he followed in his elder brother Henry's footsteps by signing for Italian club Overmach Parma and finally made his international debut in Samoa's 22–15 Rugby World Cup 2003 qualifying victory over Fiji in Nadi on 22 June 2002. He won two more caps that year, but missed out on a place in Samoa's Rugby World Cup and seemingly disappeared from view – three years passed before he pulled on a Samoan shirt for a fourth time.

It took a move to English club Leicester Tigers in 2004 to ignite his career and unlock his vast potential: he made an explosive start to life in the Guinness Premiership and quickly forged a reputation as being a devastating attacking force – scoring eight tries in eight consecutive games at one point in the season and a league record five in the match against Leeds in September 2004 – and ended the season with a Premiership winners' medal and voted the Tigers fans' Player of the Year.

It did not take long before Samoa came calling for a second time. He won his fourth cap for Samoa during their 74–7 defeat to Australia on 11 June 2005 and scored his first international tries – four of them – three weeks later during a 50–28 Rugby World Cup qualifying victory over Tonga. He featured in all five of Samoa's remaining fixtures that year – including defeats against Scotland (18–11) and England (40–3) in the 2005 autumn internationals. In 2006, he made his one, and to date only, appearance for the Pacific Islanders – a 61–17 defeat against Ireland at Lansdowne Road (his only outing in international Rugby that year) – and in 2007 played at Rugby World Cup for the first time – appearing in all four of his country's matches and scoring a try during their 25–21 victory over the United States (their only win of the Tournament).

And that seemed to be that. Tuilagi disappeared from international Rugby for the second time in his career, but continued to shine for Leicester, appearing in five domestic and continental finals for the club between 2006 and 2008. However, he was back in blue for Samoa's 2010 autumn defeats to Ireland, Scotland and England and seems certain to appear in his second Rugby World Cup in New Zealand in 2011. The Tournament will be better for his presence.

Pace coupled with raw power makes Alesana Tuilagi a feared opponent.

Felipe Contepomi Argentina

A star performer at Rugby World Cup 2007 when the Pumas proved the surprise package of the Tournament to reach the semi-finals, Felipe Contepomi is one of the most accomplished performers in world Rugby. Captain since 2008, he is equally comfortable at fly-half or inside-centre.

Felipe Contepomi made his senior international debut against Chile in October 1998, aged 21, and has been a permanent fixture in the Pumas squad ever since. He joined English club Bristol in 1999 and the same year was named in Argentina's Rugby World Cup squad, making three replacement appearances as the Pumas reached the quarter-finals for the first time. He put in some eye-catching performances for Argentina during 2001 – notably when he scored 25 points (one try, one conversion, five penalties and a drop-goal)) during the Pumas' memorable 30–16 victory over Wales at the Millennium Stadium on 20 November 2001 – and finally nailed down a place in the starting line-up. He made his second Rugby World Cup appearance in 2003, playing in all four of Argentina's pool games, and joined Irish provincial side Leinster for the 2003–04 season.

He took Irish Rugby by storm, breaking the scoring record in the Celtic League and winning legions of fans with his attacking style of play. He shone at international level, too, scoring 14 points in Argentina's 24–14 victory over France in Marseille on 20 November 2004 (France's first-ever defeat at the Stade Vélodrome) and, on 11 November 2006, nailing a drop-goal during the Pumas' first-ever Twickenham victory over England (25–18).

But it was at Rugby World Cup 2007 in France that Contepomi finally received the widespread plaudits his talent deserved. He was one of the players of the Tournament, finishing second on the points-scoring list (with 91 points) as Argentina surprised everybody by reaching the semi-finals. He ended the year named among the nominees for the IRB Player of the Year award.

He was named captain of the national side in 2008, leading a side eager to rebuild and push on from their Rugby World Cup showing. In March 2009, he announced he would be leaving Leinster at the end of the season to join French club Toulon and it seemed as though he would bow out in style, scoring all of his side's points in their 6–5 quarter-final victory over Harlequins, before suffering a serious knee injury in the semi-final against Munster.

He returned to action with Toulon in November 2009 and showed he had lost none of his attacking flair when, on 26 June 2010, he led Argentina to a thumping 41–13 home victory over France, contributing 31 points to his team's cause (with two tries, three conversions and five penalties). A much-changed Argentina may not be as strong as they were four years ago, but if they come anywhere near to repeating their 2007 performance at Rugby World Cup 2011, you can be sure that Contepomi will have played a major role.

FACTS AND FIGURES

Born:	20 August 1977, Buenos Aires, Argentina
Position:	Inside-centre, fly-half
Club:	Toulon (Fra)
Height:	1.83m (6ft)
Weight:	91.6kg (202lb)
Caps:	70
Debut:	v Chile at Santiago on 10 October 1998
Points:	557 (13t, 60c, 121p, 3dg)

Argentina's multi-talented Contepomi is one of the best in the business.

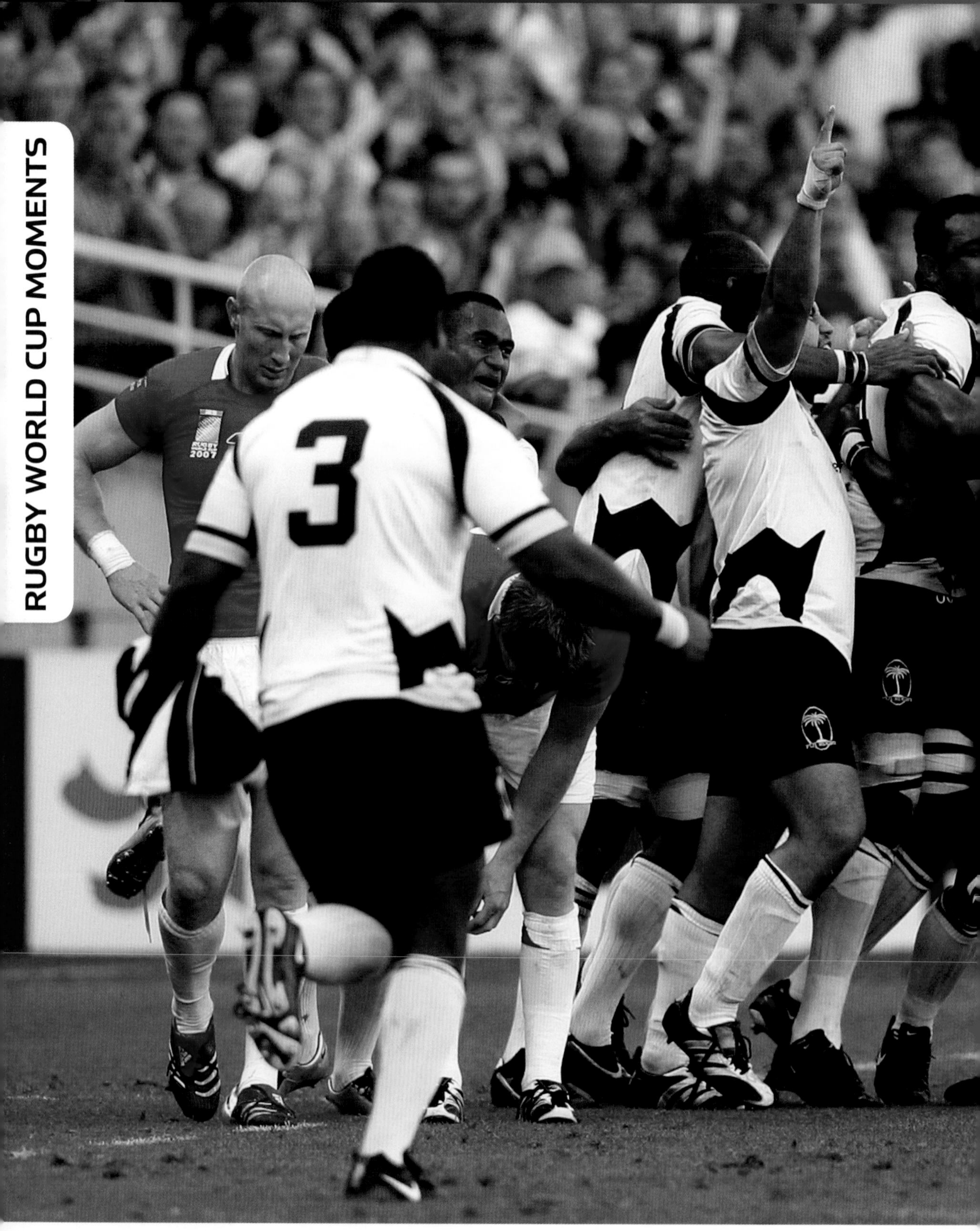
3
2007

LAST-GASP FIJI EDGE THRILLER
29 SEPTEMBER 2007, STADE DE LA BEAUJOIRE, NANTES

The stakes could not have been higher: both Fiji and Wales (with two victories and one defeat in their opening three Rugby World Cup 2007 matches) needed to win their final Pool B match to progress to the quarter-finals. Wales opened the scoring, but it was Fiji who had the better of the first half, scoring three tries and racing into a 25–3 lead. But then Fiji were reduced to 14 men for ten minutes when Akapusi Qera saw yellow and Wales roared back into contention, scoring four tries to retake the lead (29–25). Two Nicky Little penalties handed Fiji the advantage (31–29), before Martyn Williams scored a breakaway try to hand Wales a 34–31 lead with six minutes remaining. Fiji unleashed wave after wave of desperate attack before Graham Dewes crashed over for a try and Little converted to hand the islanders a pulsating victory.

Fiji celebrate certain victory while Wales' players contemplate a shock early Tournament exit.

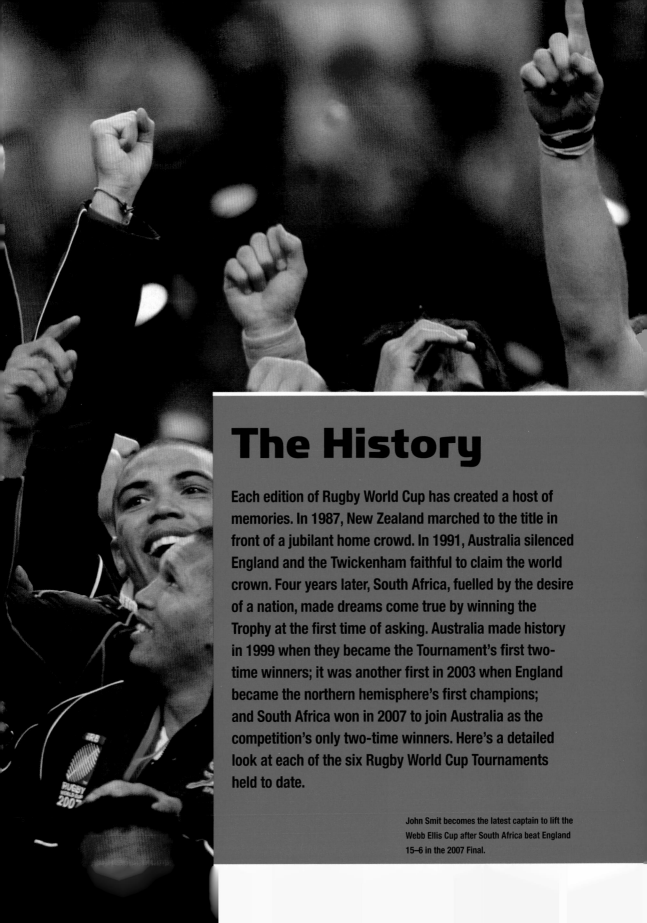

The History

Each edition of Rugby World Cup has created a host of memories. In 1987, New Zealand marched to the title in front of a jubilant home crowd. In 1991, Australia silenced England and the Twickenham faithful to claim the world crown. Four years later, South Africa, fuelled by the desire of a nation, made dreams come true by winning the Trophy at the first time of asking. Australia made history in 1999 when they became the Tournament's first two-time winners; it was another first in 2003 when England became the northern hemisphere's first champions; and South Africa won in 2007 to join Australia as the competition's only two-time winners. Here's a detailed look at each of the six Rugby World Cup Tournaments held to date.

John Smit becomes the latest captain to lift the Webb Ellis Cup after South Africa beat England 15–6 in the 2007 Final.

Great Rugby World Cup Qualifying Matches

Rugby World Cup qualifying Tournaments were introduced for the 1991 edition of the event and have since gone on to become not only an integral part of the international fixture list, but also an essential tool in spreading the Rugby gospel to the furthest reaches of the globe. It has been a successful mission: in 1991, 25 countries fought for eight qualifying places; by 2011, the number of countries had risen to 86. Here is a selection of some of the best qualifying matches in history.

Ivory Coast v Morocco v Namibia v Zimbabwe

(RUGBY WORLD CUP 1995 QUALIFYING)
14–18 June 1994, Casablanca

The 16 teams aiming to secure the one available qualifying spot in the African section for Rugby World Cup 1995 (the first and to date only time the Tournament has been staged on African soil) had been reduced to four. These were the Ivory Coast, Morocco, Namibia (the firm favourites, who were attempting to qualify for the Tournament for the first time since gaining independence from South Africa in 1991) and Zimbabwe. The quartet played each other in a round-robin group in Casablanca in June 1994. No one could have predicted the outcome. Namibia beat Zimbabwe (25–20) and Morocco beat the Ivory Coast (17–9) in the opening round of matches. Then came the turnaround: Zimbabwe beat Morocco (21–9), the Ivory Coast netted surprise victories over Namibia (13–12) and Zimbabwe (17–10) and everything hinged on the match between Morocco and Namibia, with the hosts needing to win by three points and Namibia just needing to win. It ended in a 16–16 draw and the Ivory Coast qualified for Rugby World Cup 1995 for the first, and to date only, time in their history.

Tonga v Korea

(RUGBY WORLD CUP 2003 QUALIFYING)
15 March 2003, Seoul, Korea/22 March 2003, Nuku'alofa, Tonga

It was the final round of repechage matches in the Rugby World Cup 2003 qualifying Tournament, the last-chance saloon for Tonga and Korea's hopes of securing a ticket to Australia. Tonga had suffered at the hands of their South Pacific neighbours, Fiji and Samoa, in the Oceania regional qualifying group (losing all four matches); Korea, on the other hand, had finished behind Japan in the Asian section for the third consecutive time – but this was a shot at redemption. It was a spectacularly one-sided affair: Tonga won the first leg, played in Seoul on 15 March 2003 with sublime ease, scoring 12 tries in a 75–0 rout and fared even better in the return leg in Nuku'alofa a week later, scoring 17 tries (all of them converted) to win 119–0. Tonga's 194–0 aggregate victory is an all-time record in a two-leg Rugby World Cup qualifying fixture.

Benhur Kivalu scored four of Tonga's 17 tries in a thumping 119–0 victory over Korea.

Portugal v Uruguay

(RUGBY WORLD CUP 2007 QUALIFYING)
10 March 2007, Lisbon, Portugal/24 March 2007, Montevideo, Uruguay

The final repechage round for the 2007 Tournament saw Uruguay (seeking to play in the Tournament for the third time) face off against Portugal (who had never qualified). Both sides had suffered near-misses to get there: Uruguay had lost out in the final round of qualifying in the Americas section, while Portugal had finished third in the 2004–06 European Nations Cup to miss out on one of Europe's two qualifying spots. Portugal edged the first leg in Lisbon, outscoring Uruguay by two tries to one to win 12–5 and although Uruguay scored more tries two weeks later in the return leg in Montevideo (scoring three tries to none), four penalties from Duarte Pinto kept Portugal in the match. The 18–12 final scoreline meant they won the tie by the slenderest of margins: 24–23.

Portugal overcame stiff opposition from Uruguay to qualify for Rugby World Cup 2007.

Russia v Romania

(RUGBY WORLD CUP 2011 QUALIFYING)
28 February 2009, Bucharest, Romania

European qualification for Rugby World Cup 2011 was determined through the final standings in the European Nations Cup, with the top two teams qualifying automatically and the third-place team progressing to the repechage round. The 2008–10 European Nations Cup saw Georgia romp to first place in the table, but the real story focused on the battle for second, the result of which ultimately came down to Romania's home match against Russia in February 2009. Romania may have been considered favourites, but it was Russia who stole the day, matching Romania's three tries with three of their own and adding three penalties to boot to win 29–18.

It was the result that ultimately secured Russia a first-ever visit to the Rugby World Cup. All was not lost for Romania, however, and they kept alive their proud record of appearing at every Tournament by beating Uruguay in the repechage.

RUGBY WORLD CUP QUALIFYING RECORDS

GENERAL
Most available qualifying spots:
16 for Rugby World Cup 1999

Fewest available qualifying spots:
7 for Rugby World Cup 1995

TEAM
Biggest victory:
155–3 – Japan v Chinese Taipei at Tokyo on 7 July 2002

Biggest half-time lead:
83–3 – Hong Kong v Singapore at Kuala Lumpur on 27 October 1994

Most points: 1,740 – Japan

Fewest points: 5 – Pakistan

Most points conceded: 1,469 – Korea

Fewest points conceded:
14 – Scotland

Most tries: 259 – Japan

Most matches: 50 – Spain

Most victories: 28 – Spain

Most defeats: 24 – Korea

Fewest victories: 0 – Finland, Nigeria, Pakistan, St Vincent and the Grenadines, Vanuatu

Fewest defeats: 0 – Australia, England, Ireland, Wales, Scotland

PLAYER
Most points overall:
206 – Esteban Roque Segovia (Spa)

Most points in a match:
60 – Toru Kurihara (Jap) against Chinese Taipei at Tainan on 21 July 2002

Most tries overall:
34 – Daisuke Ohata (Jap)

Most tries in a match:
10 – Ashley Billington (HK) against Singapore at Kuala Lumpur on 27 October 1994

Rugby World Cup History: The 1987 Tournament

t may have been a long time coming, but the first-ever Rugby World Cup, co-hosted by Australia and New Zealand (the originators of the idea in the early 1980s), kicked off on 22 May 1987. Sixteen teams, all invited by the IRB, contested the Tournament that ended with New Zealand beating France 29–9 in the Final to become Rugby's first World Champions.

The pool stages of the competition featured four groups of four with the top two teams progressing to the quarter-finals and if the Tournament's opening matches highlighted anything it was the gulf in class between the game's haves and have-nots. A familiar pattern started to emerge: the pool's higher-ranked teams contested what was effectively a shootout for top spot before cruising to victory in their other two games.

In Pool One, Australia started their campaign with a 19–6 win over England and eased to victory over the United States (47–12) and Japan (42–23) to win the group. England recovered from their opening-game defeat to the

Wallabies by recording their own wins over Japan (60–7) and the United States (34–6) to secure second place in the pool and a place in the last eight.

It was a familiar story in Pool Two. Wales secured a crucial 13–6 victory over Ireland and confirmed top spot in the pool with subsequent victories over Tonga (29–16) and Canada (40–9). Ireland rallied to beat Canada (46–19) and Tonga (32–9) to finish second.

Pool Three was the exception. New Zealand were the form team of the group, grinding out impressive victories over Italy (70–6 in the Tournament's opening game), Fiji (74–13) and Argentina (46–15) to top the table, and

after all the other teams had recorded one win apiece in their remaining two fixtures, it was Fiji who joined them in the quarter-finals by dint of having scored more tries (six) than either Italy (five) or Argentina (four).

Pool Four opened with a Rugby World Cup rarity, a draw (one of only two in the competition's history) between France and Scotland. The result meant the mission for both sides was to score as many tries as they could in their final two matches – against Romania and Zimbabwe – to win the pool (and, more importantly, avoid the daunting prospect of a quarter-final clash against New Zealand in Auckland). France edged the

RUGBY WORLD CUP HEROES

SERGE BLANCO (FRANCE)

There were few more graceful sights in Rugby than watching the athletic figure of Serge Blanco tearing down the touchline with ball in hand and, in careers terms, few were more successful than the Venezuela-born France full-back. A total of 93 caps in 11 years (17 as captain) and a France all-time record 38 tries bear testament to his legendary status, but no moment in his illustrious career is remembered more than his spectacular match-winning try against Australia in the dying moments of the Rugby World Cup 1987 semi-final.

battle (by 22 tries to Scotland's 20) to win the group.

The quarter-finals ran to the formbook, with each of the group winners progressing: New Zealand (thanks to a solid 30–3 victory over Scotland); Australia (who beat Ireland 33–15); France (courtesy of a 31–16 win over Fiji); and Wales (who downed England 16–3). But if the quarter-finals had generally been run-of-the-mill encounters, the semi-finals were explosive ones, with the first – Australia against France at the Concord Oval in Sydney – considered one of the greatest matches of all time. This was one of the great Australia sides, and certainly one that was expected to contest the first Rugby World Cup Final, but France, the reigning northern hemisphere champions, had other ideas, scoring a dramatic try through Serge Blanco in the game's dying moments – when it seemed the match was set for extra-time – to secure a 30–24 victory. A day later, the second semi-final between New Zealand and Wales in Auckland saw the home side, who were getting better and better with each match, produce the most impressive display of the Tournament. The All Blacks ran in eight tries (with two apiece for John Kirwan and Wayne Shelford) in an emphatic 49–6 victory. To compound Wales' disappointment, their flanker Huw Richards was sent off – the first such instance in the Tournament's history.

Lightning struck twice for Australia in the third-place playoff match as Wales scored a last-gasp try through Adrian Hadley followed by a touchline conversion from Paul Thorburn to secure a surprise 22–21 victory. But all eyes were on the first-ever Rugby World Cup Final between New Zealand and France. What promised to be an exhilarating encounter, however, turned into a one-sided affair as the All Blacks overwhelmed a strangely subdued France to win 29–9. It may not have been the dynamic denouement to the Tournament the Rugby world had been waiting for, but no one could deny that the All Blacks had been worthy winners of the inaugural Rugby World Cup.

TOURNAMENT STATISTICS

Host nations: ... Australia and New Zealand
Dates: .... 22 May–20 June 1987
Teams: 16
Matches: 32
Overall attendance: 448,318
.... (14,010 per match)

Pool 1

Team	W	D	L	F	A	Pts
Australia	3	0	0	108	41	6
England	2	0	1	100	32	4
United States	1	0	2	39	99	2
Japan	0	0	3	48	123	0

Pool 2

Team	W	D	L	F	A	Pts
Wales	3	0	0	82	31	6
Ireland	2	0	1	84	41	4
Canada	1	0	2	65	90	2
Tonga	0	0	3	29	98	0

Pool 3

Team	W	D	L	F	A	Pts
New Zealand	3	0	0	190	34	6
Fiji*	1	0	2	56	101	2
Italy	1	0	2	40	110	2
Argentina	1	0	2	49	90	2

Fiji qualified on highest number of tries scored

Pool 4

Team	W	D	L	F	A	Pts
France	2	1	0	145	44	5
Scotland	2	1	0	135	69	5
Romania	1	0	2	61	130	2
Zimbabwe	0	0	3	53	151	0

Quarter-finals

New Zealand	30–3	Scotland
Australia	33–15	Ireland
France	31–16	Fiji
Wales	16–3	England

Semi-finals

France	30–24	Australia
New Zealand	49–6	Wales

Bronze Final

Wales	22–21	Australia

THE FINAL

New Zealand 29–9 France
Tries: Jones, Kirk, Kirwan
Con: Fox
Pens: Fox (4)
Drop: Fox

Try: Berbizier
Con: Camberabero
Pen: Camberabero

LEADING POINTS SCORERS

1	126	Grant Fox (NZ)
2	82	Michael Lynagh (Aus)
3	62	Gavin Hastings (Sco)
4	53	Didier Camberabero (Fra)
5	43	Jonathan Webb (Eng)

LEADING TRY SCORERS

1=	6	Craig Green (NZ)
=	6	John Kirwan (NZ)
3=	5	Matt Burke (Aus)
=	5	Mike Harrison (Eng)
=	5	John Gallagher (NZ)
=	5	Alan Whetton (NZ)
=	5	David Kirk (NZ)

Michael Jones (centre) scored the first of New Zealand's three tries in the 1987 Final.

Rugby World Cup History: The 1991 Tournament

The second edition of Rugby World Cup, staged in the United Kingdom, France and Ireland in autumn 1991, had it all: a huge upset, adrenalin-fuelled fixtures, last-gasp tries, a missed match-saving kick and a dream Final between two old rivals. And at the end of a pulsating contest, Australia, the best team in the Tournament, walked away with the Webb Ellis Cup.

Qualifying was introduced for the 1991 Tournament, with 25 teams from five of the world's continents competing for eight places in the competition (the eight quarter-finalists from 1987 qualified automatically). The upshot of the process was that Western Samoa replaced Tonga in the 16-team line-up ... and what an impact they would make. For the second successive Tournament, teams were placed in four pools of four teams with the top two placed teams progressing to the quarter-finals.

New Zealand opened the defence of their world title impressively, beating England 18–12 at Twickenham, and eased into the last eight as group

winners after recording routine victories over the United States (46–6) and Italy (31–21). All was not lost for England, however, who won their final two pool matches to finish second in the group.

In Pool B, Scotland and Ireland opened up with victories over Japan and Zimbabwe, and then faced each other in the final pool match to decide who would top the group. Scotland, benefiting in no small part from playing at Murrayfield (a ground where they had not lost a match for three years) won the day, with a 24–15 victory.

The drama came in the opening round of matches in Pool C, not with Australia's victory over Argentina (32–19), but when

Wales met Rugby World Cup newcomers Western Samoa at Cardiff Arms Park. The Samoans put in a fearsome display and tackled Wales off the pitch to win the match 16–13 and record what still ranks as the greatest shock in the Tournament's history ... and Wales' darkest day. The Welsh may have gone on to beat Argentina (16–7), but a final-game 38–3 reverse to Australia sent them packing from the Tournament. Western Samoa beat Argentina in their final pool match to finish second in the group behind Australia.

The Tournament really came to life in the quarter-finals: Scotland saw off Western Samoa (28–6) at Murrayfield;

England, having settled on a pack-oriented approach, out-muscled and out-fought France in Paris to win 19–10; and New Zealand overcame Canada in Lille (29–13). But the pick of the last-eight matches came when Australia met Ireland in Dublin. It was a cracker of a match and, with five minutes remaining, Australia led 15–12. Then a break by the home side resulted in flanker Gordon Hamilton galloping up the touchline to score a breakaway try, and when Ralph Keyes slotted the conversion to take Ireland into an 18–15 lead, an entire nation celebrated victory … or so they thought. The game turned once again: Ireland conceded a penalty in their own 22 and, instead of taking the shot at goal to bring the scores level, Wallabies fly-half Michael Lynagh opted to run the ball. It was a match-winning decision: several phases of play later, Lynagh himself crashed over the line to secure a famous 19–18 victory.

The first semi-final, between Scotland and England at Murrayfield, was a fixture wrought with both passion and history both old and new: they were the two oldest teams in international Rugby and, only a year earlier, Scotland had memorably won the Five Nations Grand Slam showdown between the two countries at the same venue. England got the better of the Scots on this occasion, however, winning a closely fought contest – remembered as much for Gavin Hastings' last-minute penalty miss as for England's victory – 9–6. The second semi-final saw another battle between old rivals: Australia against New Zealand in Dublin, with the Wallabies taking the spoils 16–6.

The talk before the Final centred on the different approaches of the two sides: Australia with their talented backline against England's dogged, forward-dominated gameplan. As such, England's decision to throw caution to the wind and play an attacking, free-flowing game surprised many. It was a plan that backfired, however. The Wallabies scored an early try through Tony Daly and then repelled wave after wave of England attack to hang on for a 12–6 victory.

TOURNAMENT STATISTICS

Host nations: ....England, France,
........................Ireland, Scotland and Wales
Dates: ....3 October–2 November 1991
Teams: ....16 (33 qualifying)
Matches: 32
Overall attendance: 1,060,065
........................(average 33,127 per match)

Pool A

Team	W	D	L	F	A	Pts
New Zealand	3	0	0	95	39	9
England	2	0	1	85	33	7
Italy	1	0	2	57	76	5
United States	0	0	3	24	113	3

Pool B

Team	W	D	L	F	A	Pts
Scotland	3	0	0	122	36	9
Ireland	2	0	1	102	51	7
Japan	1	0	2	77	87	5
Zimbabwe	0	0	3	31	158	3

Pool C

Team	W	D	L	F	A	Pts
Australia	3	0	0	79	25	9
Western Samoa	2	0	1	54	34	7
Wales	1	0	2	32	61	5
Argentina	0	0	3	38	83	3

Pool D

Team	W	D	L	F	A	Pts
France	3	0	0	82	25	9
Canada	2	0	1	45	33	7
Romania	1	0	2	31	64	5
Fiji	0	0	3	27	63	3

Quarter-finals

England	19–10	France
Scotland	28–6	Western Samoa
Australia	19–18	Ireland
New Zealand	29–13	Canada

Semi-finals

England	9–6	Scotland
Australia	16–6	New Zealand

Bronze Final

New Zealand	13–6	Scotland

THE FINAL

Australia   12–6   England
Try: Daly   Pens: Webb (2)
Con: Lynagh
Pens: Lynagh (2)

LEADING POINTS SCORERS

1	68	Ralph Keyes (Ire)
2	66	Michael Lynagh (Aus)
3	61	Gavin Hastings (Sco)
4	56	Jonathan Webb (Eng)
5	44	Grant Fox (NZ)

LEADING TRY SCORERS

1=	6	David Campese (Aus)
=	6	Jean-Baptiste Lafond (Fra)
3=	4	Tim Horan (Aus)
=	4	Brian Robinson (Ire)
=	4	Iwan Tukalo (Sco)
=	4	Rory Underwood (Eng)

Australia's Nick Farr-Jones and David Campese celebrate victory in 1991.

Rugby World Cup History: The 1995 Tournament

Although the first two Rugby World Cups were full of drama and scintillating Rugby, the 1995 Tournament, held in South Africa and the last of the game's amateur era, is widely considered to be when the competition truly came alive. An enthralled world watched as South Africa, driven by unprecedented levels of home support, lifted the Trophy at the first time of asking.

The Tournament's opening match saw hosts South Africa overcome Australia (27–18) in Cape Town. It was a crucial victory as not only did it mean South Africa became the favourites to win Pool A, but it also instilled a sense of belief in both the South Africa squad and, more importantly, its fans. That belief only rose further when the Springboks completed efficient victories over Romania (21–8) and Canada (20–0) to top the pool, with Australia recovering to finish in second place.

England won all of their matches to top Pool B, but their victories over Argentina (24–18), Italy (27–20) and Western Samoa (44–22) had been far from pretty and a significant improvement was needed if they were to trouble Australia (in a repeat of the Rugby World Cup 1991 Final) in the quarter-finals. Western Samoa proved their 1991 performance had been no aberration by reaching the last-eight for the second Tournament in succession.

New Zealand, and in particular their giant young winger Jonah Lomu, stole the headlines in Pool C. With Lomu proving all but unstoppable, the All Blacks brushed aside Ireland (43–19) and Wales (34–9) with such brutal efficiency that, with top spot in the group all but assured, they fielded a second-string XV in their final pool match against Japan. The match was a massacre: New Zealand scored 21 tries (six of them by Marc Ellis) en route to a thumping 145–17 victory. The battle for second spot came down to Ireland's final pool match against Wales in Johannesburg, with Ireland outscoring the Welsh by three tries to two to progress (24–23).

France beat Scotland (22–19) in the final round of matches to win Pool D (with the Scots also progressing), but the main story to emerge from the group was a tragic one: during the Ivory Coast's final match of the Tournament, against Tonga, their winger Max Brito suffered a horrendous injury that left

RUGBY WORLD CUP HEROES

JONAH LOMU (NEW ZEALAND)

Jonah Lomu caused a stir when he first played for New Zealand at the 1994 Hong Kong Sevens, became the youngest-ever All Black in his debut against France in June 1994 (aged 19 years 45 days) and lifted the roof when he made his first appearance at Rugby World Cup 1995. The giant 1.96m (6ft 5in) winger, with the pace of a sprinter (he once ran 100m in 10.8 seconds) was unstoppable, scoring seven tries in the Tournament – four of them against England in the semi-finals – to become the game's first global superstar.

Jonah Lomu (right) leaves England's Tony Underwood trailing in his wake in the Rugby World Cup 1995 semi-final.

him paralysed from the neck down. The incident prompted a spell of deep introspection for the game.

France opened up the quarter-finals with an impressive 36–12 victory over Ireland and, later the same day, South Africa, to the delight of a now-believing nation, found their stride against Western Samoa, with Chester Williams running in four of the Springboks six tries in a 42–14 victory. The pick of the last-eight matches, though, came when England met Australia in Cape Town. The two evenly matched teams were locked at 22–22, with the game heading for extra-time, when Rob Andrew teased over a drop-goal in the game's dying moments to hand England a 25–22 victory. They would face New Zealand in the last four after the All Blacks saw off a resilient Scotland (48–30) in Pretoria.

The two semi-finals could not have been more different. In the first, on a waterlogged pitch in Durban, South Africa edged to a nervy 19–15 victory. The second, between New Zealand and England in Cape Town, was over after 20 minutes as Lomu bulldozed his way to three early tries (out of four in the match) to put the All Blacks out of sight. England rallied in the second half, but the 45–29 final scoreline did complete justice to New Zealand's dominance. A deflated England could not pick themselves up for the third-place playoff match against France and lost 19–9.

All the pragmatic talk before Rugby World Cup 1995 Final centred on Lomu and how South Africa would go about stopping him. But the Springboks succeeded where other teams in the Tournament had failed, slowing down New Zealand ball, denying Lomu any space and reducing the Final to a kicking contest. After 90 minutes, the two sides were locked together at 9–9; they traded a penalty each early into extra-time (12–12); and then Joel Stransky planted a right-footed drop-goal to hand the Springboks a 15–12 lead and, seconds later, the final whistle blew to confirm their victory. South Africa were the World Champions.

TOURNAMENT STATISTICS

Host nation: .... South Africa
Dates: .... 25 May–24 June 1995
Teams: .... 16 (52 qualifying)
Matches: 32
Overall attendance: 936,990
.... (average 29,281 per match)

Pool 1

Team	W	D	L	F	A	Pts
South Africa	3	0	0	68	26	9
Australia	2	0	1	87	41	7
Canada	1	0	2	45	50	5
Romania	0	0	3	14	97	3

Pool 2

Team	W	D	L	F	A	Pts
England	3	0	0	95	60	9
W Samoa	2	0	1	96	88	7
Italy	1	0	2	69	94	5
Argentina	0	0	3	69	87	3

Pool 3

Team	W	D	L	F	A	Pts
New Zealand	3	0	0	222	45	9
Ireland	2	0	1	93	94	7
Wales	1	0	2	89	68	5
Japan	0	0	3	55	252	3

Pool 4

Team	W	D	L	F	A	Pts
France	3	0	0	114	47	9
Scotland	2	0	1	149	27	7
Tonga	1	0	2	44	90	5
Ivory Coast	0	0	3	29	172	3

Quarter-finals

France	36–12	Ireland
South Africa	42–14	Western Samoa
England	25–22	Australia
New Zealand	48–30	Scotland

Semi-finals

South Africa	19–15	France
New Zealand	45–29	England

Bronze Final

France	19–9	England

THE FINAL

South Africa	15–12	New Zealand (a.e.t)
Pens: Stransky (3)		Pens: Mehrtens (3)
Drops: Stransky (2)		Drop: Mehrtens

LEADING POINTS SCORERS

1	112	Thierry Lacroix (Fra)
2	104	Gavin Hastings (Sco)
3	84	Andrew Mehrtens (NZ)
4	79	Rob Andrew (Eng)
5	61	Joel Stransky (SA)

LEADING TRY SCORERS

1=	7	Marc Ellis (NZ)
=	7	Jonah Lomu (NZ)
3=	5	Gavin Hastings (Sco)
=	5	Rory Underwood (Eng)
5=	4	Thierry Lacroix (Fra)
=	4	Adriaan Richter (SA)
=	4	Chester Williams (SA)

Joel Stransky's (centre) last-gasp drop-goal secured a famous win for South Africa.

Rugby World Cup History: The 1999 Tournament

The fourth Rugby World Cup – hosted by Wales (with England, France, Ireland and Scotland also staging matches) and the first to feature 20 teams – was, despite its convoluted format, another staggering success. After a month of competition and 41 games, Australia beat France in the Final to become the first team in history to win the Tournament twice.

The manner in which the 1995 Tournament in South Africa had captured the public's imagination was reflected in the corporate success of the 1999 edition of the Tournament: global television viewing figures passed the three-billion mark for the first time and profits from the Tournament rose from £17.6 million in 1995 to £47 million. With the Tournament entry increased for the first time to 20 teams, RWC organizers decided to place the teams in five groups of four, with the group winners guaranteed a place in the quarter-finals and the group runners-up, plus the best third-placed side, entering a round of repechage matches to decide the three final last-eight places.

Defending champions South Africa's opening-game 46–29 victory over Scotland at Murrayfield gave them the edge in Pool One, with subsequent victories over Spain (47–3) and Uruguay (39–3) guaranteeing their place in the quarter-finals. Scotland, as expected, qualified for the repechage round. There were few surprises in Pool Two, with the outcome of the group always likely to depend on the result of the England–New Zealand clash at Twickenham (both sides swept aside Tonga and Italy, the other sides in the pool, with ease). The All Blacks proved too strong for the men in white, winning 30–16. France beat Fiji into second place to top Pool Three and although hosts Wales suffered a shock at

the hands of Samoa in Pool Four (losing 31–38 in Cardiff), wins over Argentina (23–18) and Japan (64–15) were enough to win the group. Samoa and Argentina both progressed to the repechage round. As expected, Australia won Pool Five with Ireland finishing second.

And then came the extra round. England, with a young Jonny Wilkinson kicking 23 of their points, beat Fiji 45–24 at Twickenham; Scotland proved too strong for Samoa (winning a physical match 35–20); and Argentina shocked Ireland 28–24 in Lens. With the huffing and puffing finally over – and this format has not been used at a Rugby World Cup since – Rugby World Cup 1999 could begin in earnest.

Jannie de Beer's five drop-goals shocked England and handed South Africa victory in Paris in the Rugby World Cup 1999 quarter-finals.

TOURNAMENT STATISTICS

Host nation: .... Wales (with co-hosts
...... England, France, Ireland and Scotland)
Dates: ....1 October–6 November 1999
Teams: .... 20 (65 qualifying)
Matches: 41
Overall attendance: .... 1,556,572 million
.... (average 37,965 per match)

Pool 1

Team	W	D	L	F	A	Pts
South Africa*	3	0	0	132	35	9
Scotland§	2	0	1	120	58	7
Uruguay	1	0	2	42	97	5
Spain	0	0	3	18	122	0

Pool 2

Team	W	D	L	F	A	Pts
New Zealand*	3	0	0	176	28	9
England§	2	0	1	184	47	7
Tonga	1	0	2	48	171	5
Italy	0	0	3	35	196	3

Pool 3

Team	W	D	L	F	A	Pts
France*	3	0	0	108	52	9
Fiji§	2	0	1	124	68	7
Canada	1	0	2	114	82	5
Namibia	0	0	3	42	186	3

Pool 4

Team	W	D	L	F	A	Pts
Wales*	2	0	1	118	71	7
Samoa§	2	0	1	97	72	7
Argentina§	2	0	1	83	51	7
Japan	0	0	3	36	140	3

Pool 5

Team	W	D	L	F	A	Pts
Australia*	3	0	0	135	31	9
Ireland§	2	0	1	100	45	7
Romania	1	0	2	50	126	5
United States	0	0	3	52	135	3

* = qualified for quarter-finals;
§ = qualified for quarter-final playoffs

Quarter-final playoffs

England	45–24	Fiji
Scotland	35–20	Samoa
Argentina	28–24	Ireland

Quarter-finals

Australia	24–9	Wales
South Africa	44–21	England
New Zealand	30–18	Scotland
France	47–26	Argentina

Semi-finals

Australia	27–21	South Africa (aet)
France	43–31	New Zealand

Bronze Final

South Africa	22–18	New Zealand

THE FINAL

Australia	35–12	France

Tries: Tune, Finegan   **Pens:** Lamaison (4)
Cons: Burke (2)
Pens: Burke (7)

LEADING POINTS SCORERS

1	102	Gonzalo Quesada (Arg)
2	101	Matt Burke (Aus)
3	97	Jannie de Beer (SA)
4	79	Andrew Mehrtens (NZ)
5	69	Jonny Wilkinson (Eng)

LEADING TRY SCORERS

1	8	Jonah Lomu (NZ)
2	6	Jeff Wilson (NZ)
3=	4	Keith Wood (Ire)
=	4	Philippe Bernat-Salles (Fra)
=	4	Viliame Satala (Fij)
=	4	Dan Luger (Eng)

Australia exposed Wales' indifferent form in the first of the quarter-finals in Cardiff, scoring three tries (two by livewire scrum-half George Gregan and one by Ben Tune) to ease to a 24–9 victory. In Paris, South Africa fly-half Jannie de Beer produced one of the greatest kicking performances in Rugby history – nailing an extraordinary five drop-goals, five penalties and two conversions – to help his side to a convincing 44–21 win over England. New Zealand brushed aside a valiant Scotland in Edinburgh (30–18) and France defeated Argentina 47–26 in Dublin to complete the semi-final line-up.

Both semi-finals were staged at Twickenham. In the first of them, Australia faced a tense kicking encounter against a South Africa side that was short of ideas but keen to repeat the formula that had seen them to victory over England. It did not work this time round, though, and Australia

edged to a 27–21 victory after extra-time. The best match of the Tournament (and arguably in history) came in the second of the semi-finals. When New Zealand led 24–10 in the early stages of the second half, it seemed the match was running towards its pre-game script – the pre-Tournament favourites would canter to a much-expected victory. But then the French sprung into life: producing the best 20 minutes of Rugby in history, they scored 33 unanswered points before the shell-shocked All Blacks scored a consolation try in the final moments of the game. When the final whistle blew, a jubilant France had run out 43–31 winners.

But just as had been the case 12 years earlier – when France had shocked Australia in their last-four encounter – the French had reserved their best performance for the semi-finals. The Final against Australia at Cardiff's

Millennium Stadium was a damp squib of an affair, with the Wallabies running out comfortable 35–12 winners to make history: the Wallabies had become Rugby World Cup's first two-time winners.

Australia's John Eales takes the honours.

Rugby World Cup History: The 2003 Tournament

Rugby World Cup returned to Australia in 2003 and was met by a record number of fans who feasted on six weeks of exhilarating Rugby. By the time the end-of-Tournament fireworks fizzed in Sydney's night sky, England, pre-Tournament favourites and No. 1 in the rankings, lived up to their billing by beating the hosts 20–17 after extra-time in a hard-fought final.

This was the second successive Tournament with 20 teams (eight of them seeded and 12 through a qualification process that had featured a record 80 teams), although this time round the teams were placed in four groups of five teams with the top two placed teams progressing to the quarter-finals. The controversial quarter-final playoffs of 1999 had been consigned to the waste-bins of history.

Hosts Australia were the form team in Pool A, opening up first in convincing fashion, with victories over Argentina (24–8) and Romania (90–8), and then in record-breaking style, when they hammered Namibia 142–0 and scored a mind-boggling 22 tries in the process – both all-time Tournament records. It left the Wallabies facing Ireland, who had also won their opening three matches – against Romania (45–17), Namibia (64–7) and Argentina (16–15) – in the final round of the pool matches to decide who would top the pool. The Wallabies won a terrific contest 17–16, with Ireland also progressing to the last eight.

France racked up the points to top Pool B, scoring 40-plus points in all four of their matches – against Fiji (61–18), Japan (51–29), Scotland (51–9) and the United States (41–14). Scotland rallied to beat Fiji (22–20) in the final round of matches to maintain their proud record of having made it to the quarter-finals (at least) in every one of the six Rugby World Cups they have entered.

England lived up to their pre-Tournament billing by topping Pool C in an efficient fashion. They eased to victory in their opening match against Georgia (84–6), completed a crucial, group-deciding victory over South Africa (25–6), survived one or two scares to win a bruising encounter against Samoa (35–22) and rounded out the pool phase with a thumping 111–13 victory over Uruguay. In spite of their defeat to England, the Springboks won their three remaining pool games and progressed to the quarter-finals.

RUGBY WORLD CUP HEROES

CHRIS LATHAM (AUSTRALIA)

Second in Australia's all-time try-scoring charts (with 40) and third in the Rugby World Cup list (with 11), Chris Latham won 78 caps between 1998 and 2007. The fast-running full-back's most memorable day came during Australia's pool match against Namibia at Rugby World Cup 2003, when he ran in five tries during the Wallabies' thumping 142–0 victory. It was the only appearance he made in the Tournament, however, and he watched on from the sidelines as Australia lost to England in the Final.

Chris Latham scores the second of his Tournament record five tries against Namibia at Rugby World Cup 2003.

New Zealand, desperate to erase the bitter memories of their Rugby World Cup 1999 semi-final exit to France, eased to victory in their opening three pool matches – beating Italy (70–7), Canada (68–6) and Tonga (91–7) – and although they beat Wales to top the group, the 53–37 scoreline suggested one or two weaknesses in the All Blacks' armoury. Wales – their 37 points in the match against New Zealand a record for a losing team in the Rugby World Cup – joined them in the last-eight.

The quarter-finals ran to the formbook: New Zealand were too strong for South Africa, scoring three tries in a one-sided 29–9 victory; Australia beat Scotland 33–16); France had too much for Ireland (winning 43–21); and England, guided by the boot of Jonny Wilkinson with 23 points), launched a second-half recovery to see off Wales (28–17).

Australia secured the major shock of the Tournament in the first of the semi-finals in Sydney when they outplayed New Zealand to record a 22–10 victory. The second semi-final, played at the same venue a day later, saw another kicking masterclass from Wilkinson, as the young fly-half kicked all of his side's points (five penalties and three drop-goals) during England's ruthlessly efficient 24–7 victory over France.

Any thoughts England may have harboured that they would stroll to the title disappeared as early as the seventh minute, when Lote Tuqiri crossed the line to hand the Wallabies the lead. England rallied, first through the boot of Wilkinson and then through an explosive Jason Robinson try to reclaim the advantage, but Australia dug deep and after 80 minutes the scores were locked at 14–14. The sides traded penalties in extra-time to make it 17–17, and then came the decisive passage of play. England won a lineout just outside Australia's 22, drove infield and, eventually, with 26 seconds left on the clock, the ball found its way to Wilkinson, who nailed a right-footed drop-goal between the posts. Moments later the final whistle blew: England had become the new Rugby World Cup Champions.

TOURNAMENT STATISTICS

Host nation: ....Australia
Dates: ...... 10 October–22 November 2003
Teams: .... 20 (80 qualifying)
Matches: 48

Overall attendance: 1,836,607
........................(average 38,263 per match)

Pool 1

Team	W	D	L	F	A	Pts
Australia	4	0	0	273	32	18
Ireland	3	0	1	141	56	15
Argentina	2	0	2	140	57	11
Romania	1	0	3	65	192	5
Namibia	0	0	4	28	310	0

Pool 2

Team	W	D	L	F	A	Pts
France	4	0	0	204	70	20
Scotland	3	0	1	102	97	14
Fiji	2	0	2	98	114	10
United States	1	0	3	86	125	6
Japan	0	0	4	79	163	0

Pool 3

Team	W	D	L	F	A	Pts
England	4	0	0	255	47	19
South Africa	3	0	1	184	60	15
Samoa	2	0	2	138	117	10
Uruguay	1	0	3	56	255	4
Georgia	0	0	4	46	200	0

Pool 4

Team	W	D	L	F	A	Pts
New Zealand	4	0	0	282	57	20
Wales	3	0	1	132	98	14
Italy	2	0	2	77	123	8
Canada	1	0	3	54	135	5
Tonga	0	0	4	46	178	1

Quarter-finals

New Zealand	29–9	South Africa
Australia	33–16	Scotland
France	43–21	Ireland
England	28–17	Wales

Semi-finals

Australia	22–10	New Zealand
England	24–7	France

Bronze Final

New Zealand 40–13 France

THE FINAL

England	20–17	Australia (a.e.t)
Try: Robinson		Try: Tuqiri
Pens: Wilkinson (4)		Pens: Flatley (4)
Drop: Wilkinson		

LEADING POINTS SCORERS

1	113	Jonny Wilkinson (Eng)
2	103	Frédéric Michalak (Fra)
3	100	Elton Flatley (Aus)
4	75	Leon MacDonald (NZ)
5	71	Chris Paterson (Sco)

LEADING TRY SCORERS

1=	7	Doug Howlett (NZ)
=	7	Mils Muliaina (NZ)
3	6	Joe Rokocoko (NZ)
4=	5	Will Greenwood (Eng)
=	5	Chris Latham (Aus)
=	5	Josh Lewsey (Eng)
=	5	Mat Rogers (Aus)
=	5	Lote Tuqiri (Aus)

England's Martin Johnson lifts the Rugby World Cup after a thrilling Final against Australia.

Rugby World Cup History: The 2007 Tournament

By 2007, the Rugby World Cup had evolved into one of the biggest sporting Tournaments on the planet, attracting a record 2.26 million ticket sales and a cumulative global television audience of 4.2 billion. The matches duly lived up to the occasion, producing shock after shock until South Africa beat England in the Final to lift the Trophy for a second time.

Although the pool stages at previous Tournaments had, with the odd, rare exception, generally been a gentle countdown before the knockout stages, Rugby World Cup 2007 was explosive from the first whistle. Argentina shocked hosts France (17–12) to set the mood and proved their performance had been no aberration by reeling off victories against Georgia (33–3), Namibia (63–3) and Ireland (30–15) to win Pool D. France and Ireland's surprise defeats to the Pumas added extra meaning to the two countries' pool match, turning it into a shootout for the group's last quarter-final place: France, the reigning Six Nations Grand Slam champions, won the

day 25–3 and Ireland were left to ponder what might have been.

South Africa claimed top spot in Pool A, recording impressive victories against Samoa (59–7) and defending champions England (36–0), digging deep to see off Tonga (30–25) and rounding out the pool phase with a resounding 64–15 victory over the United States. England rebounded from their morale-sapping defeat to the Springboks to take the pool's second quarter-final spot.

Australia won Pool B, with four wins out of four, but the group's main headlines were reserved for the final round of matches, when Fiji played Wales to decide who would join the

Wallabies in the last eight. In a topsy-turvy encounter that saw first Fiji race into a commanding lead and then Wales produce a stirring comeback to reclaim it, Graham Dewes powered over the line in the dying moments of the game to hand Fiji a memorable 38–34 victory.

New Zealand confirmed their status as pre-Tournament favourites and the world's No. 1 ranked team by producing some thumping displays to win Pool C at a canter – beating Italy (76–14), Portugal (108–13), Scotland (40–0) and Romania (85–8). The Scots dug deep to finish second in the group, but the message from Pool C was clear: New Zealand

South Africa's Bryan Habana dazzled at Rugby World Cup 2007 with his incredible pace and try-scoring ability.

RUGBY WORLD CUP HEROES

BRYAN HABANA (SOUTH AFRICA)

A winner of the IRB U21 Rugby World Championship in 2004 (which he finished as top try-scorer), Bryan Habana made his senior debut for the Springboks against England later that year and, blessed with electric pace, soon established a reputation as one of the finest finishers in the game. But it wasn't until 2007 that Habana's name attained legendary status: he was a major factor behind South Africa's success, scoring a record-equalling eight tries in the Tournament, including four in the Springboks' opening game against Samoa.

meant business and it would take an inspirational performance from another team to stop them.

Not for the first time in Rugby World Cup history, it was misfiring France who produced the outstanding performance to end the All Blacks' hopes. The French, pilloried by their home press after their surprise opening-game reverse to Argentina, brought back memories of their 1999 semi-final win over the All Blacks by producing a stunning display to win 20–18 in Cardiff. Earlier in the day, England evoked memories of their own when they bullied Australia into submission to win what came to be known as the 'Mugging in Marseille' 12–10 – with Jonny Wilkinson, the Wallabies' chief tormentor in the 2003 final, kicking all of England's points. South Africa had too much for Fiji in the third quarter-final (winning 37–20), while Argentina's march continued with a 19–13 win over Scotland.

With their Tournament hopes now back on track, it was a passionate Stade de France that greeted France for their semi-final against England, but the 80,283 crowd were reduced to silence as early as the seventh minute when Josh Lewsey capitalized on a Damien Traille error to score the match's only try and England, aided by two penalties and a drop-goal from Wilkinson, held on to win 14–9. In the second semi-final, South Africa, who had crept into the last four with minimal fuss, ended Argentina's hopes with a comfortable 37–13 victory. The Pumas ended a successful Tournament on a high, however, when they beat France 34–10 in the third-place playoff.

All eyes switched to the final. Only 36 days earlier, England and South Africa had met in Pool A with the Springboks cantering to a 36–0 victory and although England may have bounced back from the humiliation with renewed drive and passion the question remained as to how much had they improved. The answer was not enough: South Africa won the nervy, tryless Final 15–6 to become only the second team in history (joining Australia) to lift the Webb Ellis Cup for a second time.

TOURNAMENT STATISTICS

Host nation: ....France
Dates: .... 7 September–20 October 2007
Teams: .... 20 (91 qualifying)
Matches: 48

Overall attendance: 2,245,731
.......................(average 46,786 per match)

Pool 1

Team	W	D	L	F	A	Pts
South Africa	4	0	0	189	47	19
England	3	0	1	108	88	14
Tonga	2	0	2	89	96	9
Samoa	1	0	3	69	143	5
United States	0	0	4	61	142	1

Pool 2

Team	W	D	L	F	A	Pts
Australia	4	0	0	215	41	20
Fiji	3	0	1	114	136	15
Wales	2	0	2	168	105	12
Japan	0	1	3	64	210	3
Canada	0	1	3	51	120	2

Pool 3

Team	W	D	L	F	A	Pts
New Zealand	4	0	0	309	35	20
Scotland	3	0	1	116	66	14
Italy	2	0	2	85	117	9
Romania	1	0	3	40	161	5
Portugal	0	0	4	4	209	1

Pool 4

Team	W	D	L	F	A	Pts
Argentina	4	0	0	143	33	18
France	3	0	1	188	37	15
Ireland	2	0	2	64	82	9
Georgia	1	0	3	50	111	5
Namibia	0	0	4	30	212	0

Quarter-finals

England	12–10	Australia
France	20–18	New Zealand
South Africa	37–20	Fiji
Argentina	19–13	Scotland

Semi-finals

England	14–9	France
South Africa	37–13	Argentina

Bronze Final

Argentina	34–10	France

THE FINAL

South Africa   15–6   England
Pens: Steyn,   Pens: Wilkinson (2)
Montgomery (4)

LEADING POINTS SCORERS

1	105	Percy Montgomery (SA)
2	91	Felipe Contepomi (Arg)
3	67	Jonny Wilkinson (Eng)
4	50	Nick Evans (NZ)
5	47	Jean-Baptiste Élissalde (Fra)

LEADING TRY SCORERS

1	8	Bryan Habana (SA)
2	7	Drew Mitchell (Aus)
3=	6	Doug Howlett (NZ)
=	6	Shane Williams (Wal)
5=	5	Joe Rokocoko (NZ)
=	5	Vincent Clerc (Fra)
=	5	Chris Latham (Aus)

Twelve points from the boot of Percy Montgomery edged South Africa to the title in 2007.

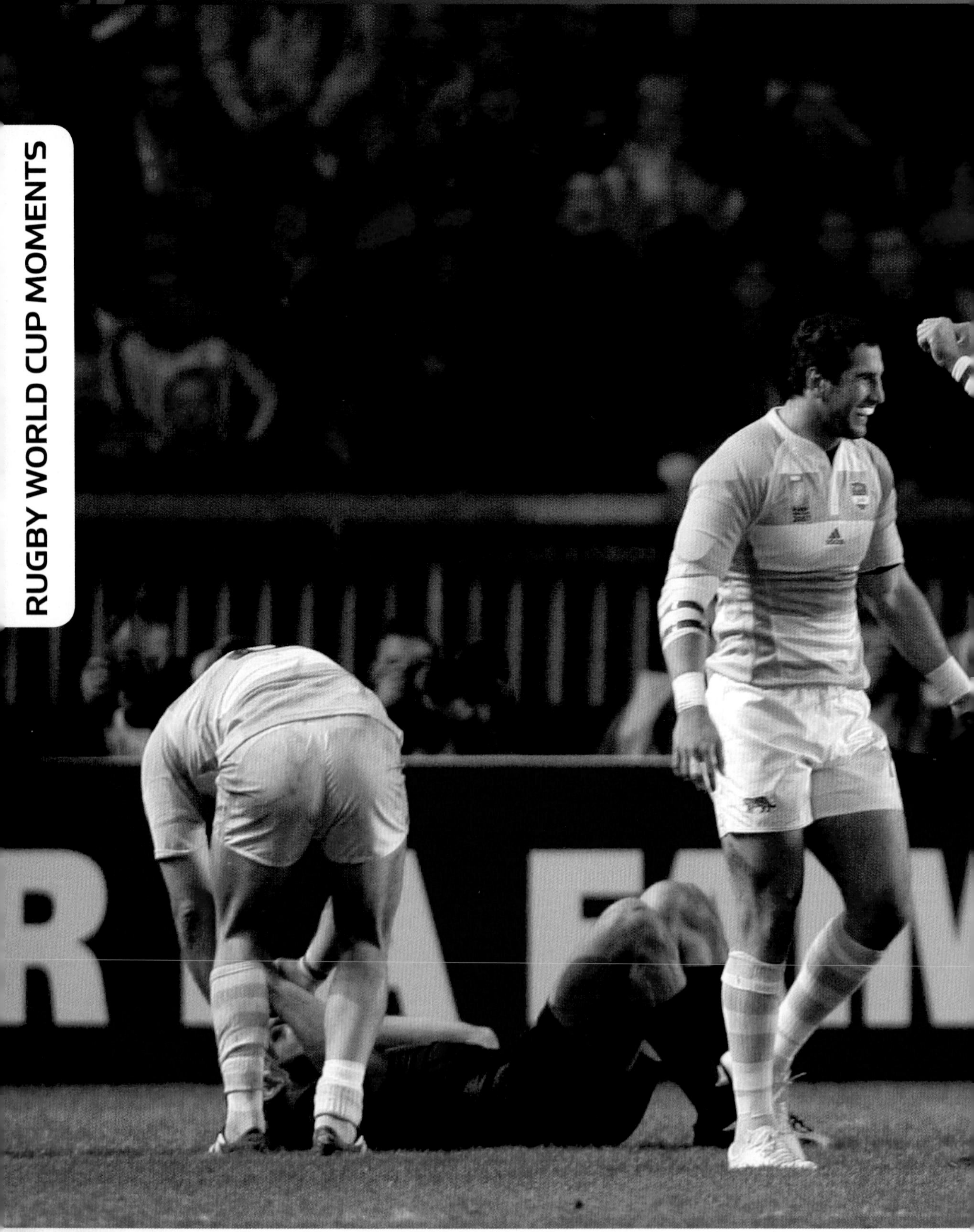

PUMAS BOW OUT IN STYLE
19 OCTOBER 2007, PARC DES PRINCES, PARIS

Far from being a run-of-the-mill affair (as is often the case in such matches when the two sides fail to pick themselves up from the disappointment of a semi-final defeat), the Rugby World Cup 2007 Bronze Final match between Argentina and France had plenty of added spice and proved to be an electric encounter. Argentina, who had beaten France in the opening match of the Tournament and had gone on to become the competition's surprise team, were desperate to bow out of what had been their best showing in a Rugby World Cup to date in style; France, on the other hand, were determined to show that their opening-game blip had been little more than an aberration. It was the Pumas, driven on by an outstanding performance from Felipe Contepomi (with 19 points in the match), who stole the day, scoring five tries to France's one to win 34–10.

Argentina celebrate their second victory over hosts France at Rugby World Cup 2007.

FACTS & STATS

A total of 2,076 players from 24 different countries in five of the Earth's continents have played in the 233 Rugby World Cup matches contested to date and among those numbers there have been plenty of record-breaking moments. What is the biggest winning margin in the Tournament's history? When was the first draw? Which team have recorded the most victories? Who is the Tournament's all-time leading points-scorer? Who holds the record for the most points in a Tournament? Which player has scored the most tries overall, in a match or in a single Tournament? Who has contested the most Rugby World Cup matches? Who was shown the Tournament's first red card? The answers to these and many more questions can be found in the following pages.

Australia's David Campese scored ten tries in 15 Rugby World Cup matches between 1987 and 1995.

TEAM RECORDS

Biggest victories: top five

Pos	Score	Winner	Opponent	Venue	Date
1	142–0	Australia	Namibia	Adelaide	25 Oct 2003
2	145–17	New Zealand	Japan	Bloemfontein	4 Jun 1995
3	101–3	New Zealand	Italy	Huddersfield	14 Oct 1999
4	111–13	England	Uruguay	Brisbane	2 Nov 2003
5	108–13	New Zealand	Portugal	Lyon	15 Sep 2007

Most wins: 30 New Zealand

Most defeats: 18 Japan

Fewest wins: 0 Ivory Coast, Namibia, Portugal, Spain and Zimbabwe

Most matches without a win:
11 Namibia between 1999 and 2007

Most tries overall: 232 New Zealand

Most points overall: 1,711 New Zealand

Most tries in a match:
22 Australia against Namibia in 2003

Most points in a match:
145 New Zealand against Japan in 1995

Most tries in a single Tournament:
52 New Zealand in 2003

Most points in a single Tournament:
361 New Zealand in 2003

Fewest points in a single Tournament:
14 Romania in 1995

Only team to have played at Rugby World Cup and not scored a try: Spain

Most points scored in a losing cause:
37 Wales in their 37–53 quarter-final defeat to New Zealand in 2003

Most tries scored in a losing cause:
5 Wales in their 34–38 defeat to Fiji in Nantes in 2007

Teams failing to score a single point

Score	Team	Opponent	Venue	Date
0–89	Ivory Coast	Scotland	Rustenberg	26 May 1995
0–20	Canada	South Africa	Port Elizabeth	3 Jun 1995
0–48	Spain	Scotland	Murrayfield	16 Oct 1999
0–142	Namibia	Australia	Adelaide	25 Oct 2003
0–36	England	South Africa	Paris	14 Sep 2007
0–42	Romania	Scotland	Murrayfield	18 Sep 2007
0–40	Scotland	New Zealand	Murrayfield	23 Sep 2007
0–30	Namibia	Georgia	Lens	26 Sep 2007

Games decided by a single point

Score	Winner	Opponent	Venue	Date
22–21	Wales	Australia	Rotorua	18 Jun 1987
19–18	Australia	Ireland	Dublin	20 Oct 1991
24–23	Ireland	Wales	Johannesburg	4 Jun 1995
19–18	Fiji	USA	Brisbane	15 Oct 2003
16–15	Ireland	Argentina	Adelaide	26 Oct 2003
17–16	Australia	Ireland	Melbourne	1 Nov 2003

Drawn matches

Score	Team 1	Team 2	Venue	Date
20–20	France	Scotland	Christchurch	23 May 1987
12–12	Canada	Japan	Bordeaux	25 Sept 2007

TRY-SCORING RECORDS

Most tries overall: top ten

Pos	Tries	Player (country, span)
1	15	Jonah Lomu (NZ, 1995–99)
2	13	Doug Howlett (NZ, 2003–07)
3=	11	Chris Latham (Aus, 1999–2007)
=	11	Joe Rokocoko (NZ, 2003–07)
=	11	Rory Underwood (Eng, 1987–95)
6=	10	David Campese (Aus, 1987–95)
=	10	Brian Lima (Sam, 1991–2007)
8=	9	Gavin Hastings (Sco, 1987–95)
=	9	Jeff Wilson (NZ, 1995–99)
10=	8	Christophe Dominici (Fra, 1999–2007)
=	8	Bryan Habana (SA, 2007))
=	8	Mils Muliaina (NZ, 2003–07)

Leading try-scorers: by Tournament

Year	Player (country)	Tries
1987	Craig Green (NZ)	6
	John Kirwan (NZ)	6
1991	David Campese (Aus)	6
	Jean-Baptiste Lafond (Fra)	6
1995	Marc Ellis (NZ)	7
	Jonah Lomu (NZ)	7
1999	Jonah Lomu (NZ)	8
2003	Doug Howlett (NZ)	7
	Mils Muliaina (NZ)	7
2007	Bryan Habana (SA)	8

Most tries in a match:
6 Marc Ellis (NZ) against Japan at Bloemfontein in 1995

Most tries in a single Tournament:
8 Jonah Lomu (NZ) in 1999; and Bryan Habana (SA) in 2007

First-ever Rugby World Cup try:
A penalty try for New Zealand against Italy in the opening match of the 1987 Tournament

Most matches played without scoring a try:
22 Jason Leonard (Eng) between 1991 and 2003

Youngest try-scorer: Terunori Masuho (Jap) was 19 years 107 days old when he scored two tries against Zimbabwe at Belfast on 14 October 1991

Oldest try-scorer: Diego Ormaechea (Uru) was 40 years 13 days old when he touched down against Spain at Galashiels on 2 October 1999

POINTS-SCORING RECORDS

Most points overall: top ten

Pos	Points	Player (country, span)
1	249	Jonny Wilkinson (Eng, 1999–2007)
2	227	Gavin Hastings (Sco, 1987–95)
3	195	Michael Lynagh (Aus, 1987–95)
4	170	Grant Fox (NZ, 1987–91)
5	163	Andrew Mehrtens (NZ, 1995–99)
6	135	Gonzalo Quesada (Arg, 1999–2003)
7=	125	Matt Burke (Aus, 1995–2003)
=	125	Nicky Little (Fij, 1999–2007)
9	124	Thierry Lacroix (Fra, 1991–95))
10	120	Gareth Rees (Can, 1987–99)

Most points in a match:
45 Simon Culhane (NZ)
    against Japan in 1995

Most points in a Tournament:
126 Grant Fox (NZ) in 1987

Most penalties overall:
53 Jonny Wilkinson (Eng)

Most penalties in a match:
8 Gavin Hastings (Sco) against Tonga
    at Pretoria on 30 May 1995;
    Thierry Lacroix (Fra) against Ireland
    at Durban on 10 June 1995;
    Gonzalo Quesada (Arg) against Samoa
    at Llanelli on 10 October 1999; and
    Matt Burke (Aus) against South Africa
    at Twickenham on 30 October 1999

Most penalties in a Tournament:
31 Gonzalo Quesada (Arg) in 1991

Most conversions overall:
39 Gavin Hastings (Sco)

Most conversions in a match:
20 Simon Culhane (NZ) against Japan
    at Bloemfontein in 1995

Most conversions in a Tournament:
30 Grant Fox (NZ) in 1987

Most drop-goals overall:
13 Jonny Wilkinson (Eng)

Most drop-goals in a match:
5 Jannie de Beer (SA) against England
    at the Stade de France in 1999

Most drop-goals in a Tournament:
8 Jonny Wilkinson (Eng) in 2003

Most points scored by a player in a losing cause:
24 David Humphreys for Ireland during their
    24–28 defeat to Argentina in 1999

Most points scored by a replacement in a match:
13 Nicky Little for Fiji during their 41–13
    victory over Japan in 2003

Leading points-scorers: by Tournament

Year	Player (country)	Points
1987	Grant Fox (NZ)	126
1991	Ralph Keyes (Ire)	68
1995	Thierry Lacroix (Fra)	112
1999	Gonzalo Quesada (Arg)	102
2003	Jonny Wilkinson (Eng)	113
2007	Percy Montgomery (SA)	105

APPEARANCE RECORDS

Most appearances: top ten

Pos	App	Player (country, span)
1	22	Jason Leonard (Eng, 1991–2003)
2	20	George Gregan (Aus, 1995–2007)
3	19	Mike Catt (Eng, 1995–2007)
4=	18	Raphael Ibanez (Fra, 1999–2007)
=	18	Martin Johnson (Eng, 1995–2003)
=	18	Brian Lima (Sam, 1991–2007)
7=	17	Lawrence Dallaglio (Eng, 1999–2007)
=	17	Sean Fitzpatrick (NZ, 1987–95)
9=	16	Os du Randt (SA, 1995–2007)
=	16	Fabien Pelous (Fra, 1999–2007)
=	16	Phil Vickery (Eng, 1999–2007)

Oldest player:
Diego Ormaechea (Uru) was 40 years 26 days
old when he played against South Africa in
1999

Youngest player:
Thretton Palamo (USA) was 19 years 8 days old
when he played against South Africa in 2007

Youngest player in a final:
Jonah Lomu (NZ) was 20 years 43 days old
when he played against South Africa in the
1995 Final

Youngest Rugby World Cup winner:
François Steyn was 20 years 159 days old
when South Africa won the Tournament in 2007

Most appearances on the losing side:
11 Romeo Gontineac (Rom)

Two-time Rugby World Cup winners:
Dan Crowley, John Eales, Tim Horan,
Phil Kearns and Jason Little for Australia
in 1991 and 1999; and Os du Randt
for South Africa in 1995 and 2007

Most appearances as captain:
11 Will Carling (Eng),
    between 1991 and 1995;
    Raphael Ibanez (Fra),
    between 1999 and 2007;
    Martin Johnson (Eng),
    between 1999 and 2003

England's Jonny Wilkinson leads Rugby World Cup's all-time points-scoring list with 249 points.

Number of red cards: by country
3   Canada, Tonga
2   South Africa
1   Argentina, Australia, Fiji,
    Namibia, Samoa, Wales

Rugby World Cup's first red card:
Huw Richards (Wal) against New Zealand
in the 1987 semi-final

Most red cards in a match:
3   South Africa (John Dalton) against Canada
    (Gareth Rees and Rod Snow)
    at Port Elizabeth in 1995

Number of yellow cards: by country
7   Tonga
6   Fiji, France
4   Argentina, Italy, Georgia,
    South Africa, USA
3   Australia, Ireland, New Zealand
2   Canada, England, Romania,
    Samoa, Scotland, Wales
1   Namibia, Portugal

Most yellow cards in a match:
3   Tonga (Ipolito Fenukitau and Milton
    Ngauamo) against Italy (Fabio Ongaro) at
    Canberra on 15 October 2003; United States
    (Paul Emerick and Vaha Esikia) against
    England (Lawrence Dallaglio) at Lens on 8
    September 2007; South Africa (Bryan Habana
    and François Steyn) against Tonga (Sefa Vaka)
    at Lens on 22 September 2007;
    Argentina (Rimas Alvarez Kairelis and Juan
    Manuel Leguizamón) against France (Raphael
    Ibanez) at Parc des Princes, Paris, on 19
    October 2007

Most yellow cards received
by a player overall:
2   Paul Emerick (USA);
    Raphael Ibanez (Fra); and
    Fabio Ongaro (Ita)

Most yellow cards for a team that
has gone on to win the match:
2   Wales (Colin Charvis and Sonny Parker)
    during their 41–10 victory over
    Canada in 2003;
    Australia (Drew Mitchell and Nathan Sharpe)
    during their 32–20 win over Wales in 2007;
    South Africa (Bryan Habana and François
    Steyn) during their 30–25 victory over
    Tonga in 2007; and
    Argentina (Rimas Alvarez Kairelis and
    Juan Manuel Leguizamón) during the
    Pumas' 34–10 third-place playoff victory
    over France in 2007

Rugby World Cup Final referees: by
Tournament

Year	Referee (country)
1987	Kerry Fitzgerald (Aus)
1991	Derek Bevan (Wal)
1995	Ed Morrison (Eng)
1999	Andre Watson (SA)
2003	Andre Watson (SA)
2007	Alain Rolland (Ire)

Most matches as referee:
11 Jim Fleming (Sco)

Number of referees: by country
8   Australia, England
7   New Zealand
6   Wales, Ireland
5   France, South Africa
3   Scotland
2   Argentina
1   Canada, Fiji, Japan, Samoa,
    South Korea, United States
Note: 56 referees have officiated
      Rugby World Cup's 233 matches

Rugby World Cup-winning coaches: by
Tournament

Year	Coach (country)
1987	Brian Lochore (NZ)
1991	Bob Dwyer (Aus)
1995	Kitch Christie (SA)
1999	Rod Macqueen (Aus)
2003	Clive Woodward (Eng)
2007	Jake White (SA)

First to play at one Rugby World Cup
and coach a team in another:
Daniel Dubroca, who played for France in 1987
and coached Les Bleus at the 1991 Tournament

Most Tournaments as coach:
3   Jim Telfer for Scotland
    in 1991, 1995 and 1999;
    Bryan Williams for Samoa
    in 1991, 1995 and 1999

Number of coaches: by country
17 New Zealand
9   France
8   Australia
7   Argentina, England
5   South Africa
4   Japan
3   Ireland, United States, Wales
2   Canada, Romania, Scotland,
    Tonga, Uruguay
1   Fiji, Georgia, Italy, Ivory Coast,
    Namibia, Portugal, Spain

Player with one team and
coach of two different teams:
John Kirwan, who played for New Zealand
at Rugby World Cup 1987 and 1991 and
then coached Italy (in 2003) and Japan
(in 2007); and Pierre Berbizier, who played
for France at Rugby World Cup 1987 and
then went on to coach France (in 1995)
and Italy (in 2007).

Coaching the defending champions:
The best result achieved by a coach leading
the defending champions into a Rugby World
Cup is to a runners-up finish – by Eddie Jones
with Australia in 2003; and Brian Ashton with
England in 2007. The worst performance is
to reach the quarter-finals – by Bob Dwyer
with Australia in 1995

Rugby World Cup host nations: by Tournament

Year	Host/s
1987	Australia, New Zealand
1991	England, France, Ireland, Scotland, Wales
1995	South Africa
1999	Wales, England, France, Ireland, Scotland
2003	Australia
2007	France

Rugby World Cup Final venues: by Tournament

Year	Venue
1987	Eden Park, Auckland
1991	Twickenham, London
1995	Ellis Park, Johannesburg
1999	Millennium Stadium, Cardiff
2003	Telstra Stadium, Sydney
2007	Stade de France, Paris

Average match attendance: by Tournament

Year	Av. per match	Total spectators	No. of matches
1987	14,010	448,318	32
1991	33,127	1,060,065	32
1995	29,281	936,990	32
1999	37,965	1,556,572	41
2003	38,263	1,836,607	48
2007	46,786	2,245,731	48

Highest match attendances: top five

Pos	Spectators	Match	Venue	Date
1	82,957	Australia v England	Telstra Stadium, Sydney	22 Nov 2003
2	82,444	Australia v New Zealand	Telstra Stadium, Sydney	15 Nov 2003
3	82,346	England v France	Telstra Stadium, Sydney	16 Nov 2003
4	80,430	England v South Africa	Stade de France, Paris	20 Oct 2007
5	80,283	France v England	Stade de France, Paris	13 Oct 2007

Longest and shortest Rugby World Cups:

The longest World Cup (by days) is 43 both the 2003 (10 Oct–22 Nov 2003) and 2007 (7 Sep–22 Oct 2007) Tournaments. The shortest World Cup was the first, in 1987, which lasted 29 days (22 May–20 Jun 1987)

Lowest match attendances: top five

Pos	Spectators	Match	Venue	Date
1=	3,000	Tonga v Ireland	Brisbane	3 Jun 1987
=	3,000	USA v Romania	Lansdowne Road, Dublin	9 Oct 1999
=	3,000	Uruguay v South Africa	Hampden Park, Glasgow	15 Oct 1999
4	3,761	Spain v Uruguay	Galashiels	2 Oct 1999
5	4,000	Zimbabwe v France	Eden Park, Auckland	2 Jun 1987

Only stadium to have hosted a match at every stage of the Rugby World Cup:

Stade de France, Paris, hosted pool matches in 2007, a quarter-final in 1999 (England v South Africa) and both semi-finals and the Final in 2007

Most matches hosted (by country)

Pos	Matches	Country	(span)
1=	58	Australia	(1987–2003)
=	58	France	(1991–2007)
3	32	South Africa	(1995)
4	22	New Zealand	(1987)
5	20	Wales	(1991–2007)
6	16	England	(1991–99)
7	15	Scotland	(1991–2007)
8	12	Ireland	(1991–99)

Most matches hosted (by stadium): top ten

Pos	Matches	Stadium	(years)
1	13	Murrayfield, Edinburgh	(1991, 1999, 2007)
2	11	Millennium Stadium, Cardiff	(1999, 2007)
3	10	Twickenham, London	(1991, 1999)
4=	9	Lansdowne Road, Dublin	(1991, 1999)
=	9	Suncorp Stadium, Brisbane	(2003)
6	8	Stade de France, Paris	(1999, 2007)
7=	7	Telstra Stadium, Sydney	(2003)
=	7	Telstra Dome, Melbourne	(2003)
9=	6	Parc des Princes, Paris	(1991, 2007)
=	6	Stade Vélodrome, Marseille	(2007)

The RWC 2003 Final between Australia and England at Sydney's Telstra Stadium attracted the Tournament's biggest-ever crowd: 82,957.

The Webb Ellis Cup

At the beginning of 1987, a few months before the inaugural Rugby World Cup kicked off in Auckland and Sydney, a beautifully crafted silver Trophy stood in the vaults of its makers, Garrards, the Royal Jewellers, in Regents Street, London.

Made in 1906, this fine Trophy was a reproduction of a piece believed to have been made around 1740 by Paul de Lamerie, a Huguenot silversmith. Made of sterling silver, gilded in gold, the Trophy is adorned by a satyr head on one of the two cast scroll handles and a nymph's head on the other. The decorative features include a bearded mask, a lion mask and a vine. The Rugby World Cup 1987 Organising Committee decided that this should be the Trophy that would go on to become one of the iconic symbols of world sport. They called it The Webb Ellis Cup after the Victorian schoolboy William Webb Ellis who, legend has it, in disregard for the rules of football, picked up the ball and ran with it, thus creating the Game of Rugby.

The Cup started its march towards legend on 22 May 1987 with the RWC opening match between New Zealand and Italy and acquired immortality on 20 June at Eden Park, Auckland, when New Zealand captain David Kirk hoisted it above his head in triumph.

Since then the Trophy has travelled the world. It has been touched by royalty and Aborigine bushmen, Maori warriors and French farmers and African children and Canadian Mounties. It has acquired personality and symbolic value in the hands of winning captains. In 1995, it was given iconic status by former South African President Nelson Mandela who presented it to his winning captain, François Pienaar. It continues to be an inspiration to every player who dreams of Rugby World Cup glory.

Growing the Global Game

When the first Rugby World Cup took place in New Zealand and Australia in 1987, few would have predicted what a global success the Tournament would become. But 20 years on, Rugby World Cup has flourished into one of the world's premier sporting events.

At France 2007, over two million people attended at least one of the 48 matches, while over four billion people watched the drama unfold in over 200 broadcast territories (compared to 230 million in 17 territories in 1987), taking Rugby to new countries and markets for the first time.

Such worldwide success resulted in RWC 2007 making a surplus of £122m, meaning that cash is available for the IRB to invest across its 117 Member Unions. Indeed, 95 percent of all money distributed by the IRB worldwide for development comes from RWC revenue.

The purpose of such widespread investment is to grow the Game through a more competitive RWC. By RWC 2015 in England the IRB wants to see more teams in with a chance of lifting the Cup, through a £79 million strategic investment programme (2005–12) aimed specifically at assisting the smaller (Tier 2) Unions. These are exciting times.

The IRB is hopeful that Tier 2 Unions will be able to close the performance gap to Tier 1 Unions during Rugby World Cup 2011 in New Zealand. However, by 2015 (and certainly by 2019), it wants a lot more uncertainty as to who will lift the Webb Ellis Cup.

Credits

The publishers would like to thank the following sources for their kind permission to reproduce the pictures in this book:

Getty Images: /Simon Bruty: 17C; /Jean-Pierre Clatot/AFP: 44, 45T; /Mark Dadswell: 127; /Arnold H Drapkin/Time & Life Pictures: 24; /Alexander Fedorov/Epilson: 70, 71B; /Franck Fife/AFP: 42; /Julian Finney: 69B; /Stu Forster: 45B, 57B; /Pascal Guyot/AFP: 52; /Richard Heathcote: 73B; /Philippe Huguen/AFP: 85T; /Martin Hunter: 19B, 88–89; /Hannah Johnston: 20B; /Koichi Kamoshida: 49B; /Junko Kimura: 28–29; /Nick Koudis/Photodisc: 25T; /Patrick Kovarik/AFP: 47B; /Jean-Philippe Ksiazek/AFP: 59T; /Hideo Kurihara/Stone: 23B; /Ross Land: 109; /Warren Little: 69T; /Alex Livesey: 49T, 67B, 79T, 79B; /Jamie McDonald: 57T; /Marty Melville: 20T, 21T; /Daniel Mihailescu/AFP: 60; /Frank Perry/AFP: 80; /Harley Peters: 19T; /Dean Purcell: 21B, 106; /David Rogers: 58, 91, 94, 97; /Jochen Schlenker/Robert Harding: 2s5B; /Jochen Schlenker/Photographers Choice: 10–11; /Ross Setford: 46; /Cameron Spencer: 65T; /Luke Walker/Gallo Images: 99; /Jeff Zelevansky: 71T.

Press Association Images: 16B, 110; /ABACA: 98; /AP: 26–27, 108; /Barry Aldworth/Sports Inc: 77T; /Mark Baker/AP: 61T, 65B; /Julien Behal: 67T, 72; /Lionel Cironneau/AP: 12, 38–39, 55B; /Steve Cuff: 117; /David Davies: 53T, 64, 76, 83T, 86–87, 92, 116, 119, 125; /Anthony Devlin: 59B; /Matt Dunham/AP: 104–105; /Mike Egerton: 17B, 41T, 54, 55T, 56, 66, 82, 90, 96, 100, 112; /Vadim Ghirda/AP: 33B, 85B; /Nicolas Gouhier/ABACA: 93; /Christophe Guibbaud/ABACA: 101; /Themba Hadebe/AP: 15; /Tim Hales/AP: 78; /Marcelo Hernandez/AP: 107; /Tom Hevezi: 74–75; /Itsuo Inouye/AP: 31; /David Jones: 7, 50–51, 95; /Ross Kinnaird: 62–63, 113, 122–123; /Sheri Lamb/The Canadian Press: 32; /Tony Marshall: 40, 43T, 68, 114; /Andrew Matthews: 81B; /Toby Melville: 115; /Angela Merker/DPA: 23T; /Francois Mori/AP: 77B, 118, 120–121; /Don Morley: 16T; /Peter Morrison/AP: 41B, 48, 53B; /Claude Paris/AP: 43B, 61B; /Photomig/AP: 33T; /Stephen Pond: 83B; /Stephane Reix/ABACA: 37; /David Rogers/AP: 30; /Nousha Salimi/AP: 73T; /Ross Setford/RWC: 17T; /Neal Simpson: 47T, 111; /Mehdi Taamallah/ABACA: 102–103; /Sang Tan/AP: 14; /David Vincent/AP: 81T; /Huang Xingwei/Landov: 22. **Republikein:** 84. **Rugby World Cup Limited 1986-2011:** 4, 9, 128.

Every effort has been made to acknowledge correctly and contact the source and/or copyright holder of each picture and Carlton Books Limited apologises for any unintentional errors or omissions, which will be corrected in future editions of this book.